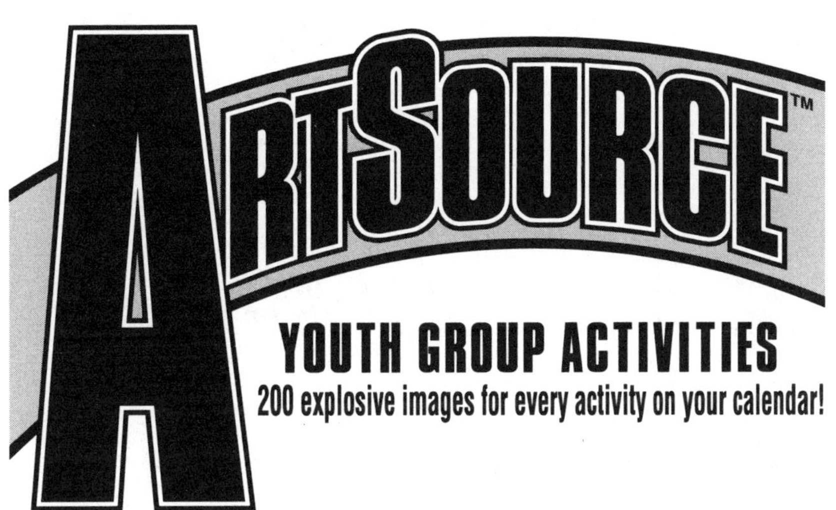

Created by Church Art Works™

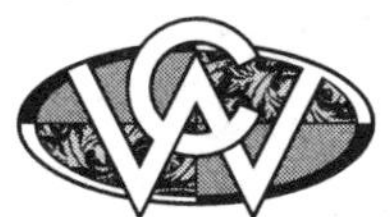

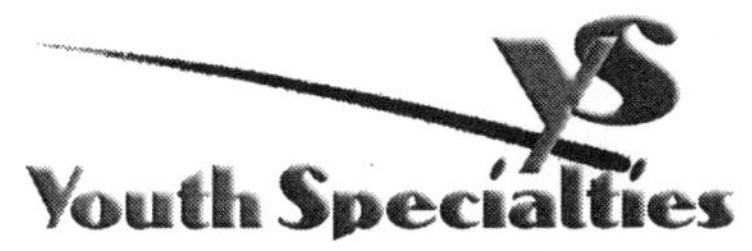

ZondervanPublishingHouse
Grand Rapids, Michigan
A Division of HarperCollins*Publishers*

ArtSource: Youth Group Activities

Youth Specialties Books, 300 S. Pierce St., El Cajon, CA 92020, are published by Zondervan Publishing House, 5300 Patterson Ave. S.E., Grand Rapids, MI 49530.

ISBN 0-310-23057-8

Created by Church Art Works™, 890 Promontory Place SE, Salem, OR 97302-1716

Printed in the United States of America

99 00 01 02 03 04 05 06 07 / / 10 9 8 7 6 5 4 3 2 1

TABLE OF CONTENTS

ACKNOWLEDGMENTS

Thanks to the hundreds of youth ministers who have submitted ideas for these illustrations. Thanks also to the artists who contributed to this book:

Dave Adamson
Dave Baker
Krieg Barrie
Mike Bartlett
Dave Bramson
Shane Cawthon
Bruce Day
Chris England
Von Glitschka
William Haffner
"Tito" Moore
John Nissen
Michelle Seefeldt
Wanda Vinje

And thanks to our support team at Church Art Works™:

Bruce Bottorff
Steve Hunt
Tony Knight
Toni Taylor
Elizabeth Wright
Ellen Zarfas
Nelson Zarfas

INTRODUCTION

We've designed ArtSource to be a quick and complete clip art sourcebook for your youth program and promotions. It contains ministry clip art from Church Art Works and other contributing artists. This ArtSource volume contains radical clips of tons of youth group activities. You can clip or photocopy art from this book to drop into the flier you're pasting together... scan it for the newsletter you're designing on computer...or pack the book off with you to a creative brainstorming session. The ideas it can spark are endless.

This book can be a valuable, time-saving asset to your ministry. You can help us with ideas for more clip art by using the Brainstorm Form on page 139. When you submit your ideas to us, you keep the creativity flowing – which assists thousands of youth workers in attracting students to their ministries and events.

LET'S BE CREATIVE!

This volume of ArtSource clip art gives you the chance to pump more life into your promotions and create excitement in your group. We suggest this approach:

1. CREATE AN EXCITING IDEA. *Advance planning and scheduling of your youth group activities is essential. But don't stop there. Hold separate brainstorming sessions to allow time for creativity to blossom. Creative ideas don't come easily in a board-meeting format, so get away to neutral territory of some sort with a few crazy idea people. Call it a Creativity Retreat, a Brain Drain, a Skull Session, or whatever you want. Let the clip art in this book inspire some new ideas, too. Get the ideas on paper and save the sorting out and logistics for later – the dates, the costs, the division of labor, etc., can wait until you get back in your office. A Creativity Retreat (or whatever you call it) helps you break away from everyday pressures in order to birth fresh ideas.*

BASIC STEPS IN PREPARING PRINTED MATERIALS

Yes, this is the age of computers and desktop publishing. And certainly you could (and should) buy ArtSource on CD and set up your whole project electronically. Sometimes, though, it's fun (and even faster) to put together your piece the Old School way. If you choose this route, you'll need a few tools: scissors, X-Acto (or craft) knife, ruler, light blue pencil (nonreproducing) for layout, glue stick or tape, black markers (with felt tips of various widths), T-square, triangles, technical pen, and drafting table or drawing board. All of these tools are available at an art or drafting store.

Photocopy or cut out pieces of art from this book for your project. You can reduce it or enlarge it on a photocopier. Choose art that fits your subject matter.

Plan your layout. Sketch (on a separate piece of paper) where you want art and where you want copy (headlines and details). See pages 9-12 for ideas.

Use felt-tip pens or a computer to set and size your type. Assemble this in combination with the clip art and paste it on a clean white sheet or card to make your master.

Photocopy the master to reproduce as many printed pieces as you need for your event.

2. CREATE AN EXCITING MESSAGE. *When you prepare your promotional piece, think like a teenager. Don't be trapped into listing just time, date, and place. Take a look at our "Hot Tips" on pages 9-12.*

3. CREATE AN EXCITING LOOK. *Think beyond the typical flier or announcement. Teenagers love the unusual. So instead of aligning things in straight lines, for example, place them at different angles on the page. Or if you usually use small type, think BIG TYPE. If you tend to illustrate your message with a normal-looking teenager (whatever that is), use a robot instead!*

One way to avoid getting trapped into the same old layout procedure is to first place the clip art on a big blank sheet, then work the headlines and copy around the clip art. Let the design be as big as you want, as long as it's fun and has impact. Working copy around the clip art (instead of the traditional order of laying out copy first, then filling in the blanks with clip art) creates unusual, attention-getting shapes and column widths. Plus it's easier to lay out – not to mention more fun!

Or use a big sheet of paper to roughly sketch out small layout options – two or three inch versions. Explore radically different layouts of the elements in your piece. For example, in one sketch the art may be huge and the type small; in another, the type may be huge and the art sized fairly small. You have many different options with the same piece of clip art – such as repeating it several times for a dramatic effect.

4. CREATE AN EXCITING ATTITUDE. *After committing your plans to God, promoting your event is the first step toward contacting those you want to reach. Stretch yourself and strive for the very best. This new attitude will be reflected in your work. Others will sense your desire for creativity and professionalism, and the enthusiasm will spread. As more people become involved in the project, you'll also stretch them. The results? Excitement as your team begins to focus on a worthwhile goal!*

In the next few pages we've given you creative examples of ways to use clip art. Use these ideas to launch your own exciting promotional pieces. Go nuts!

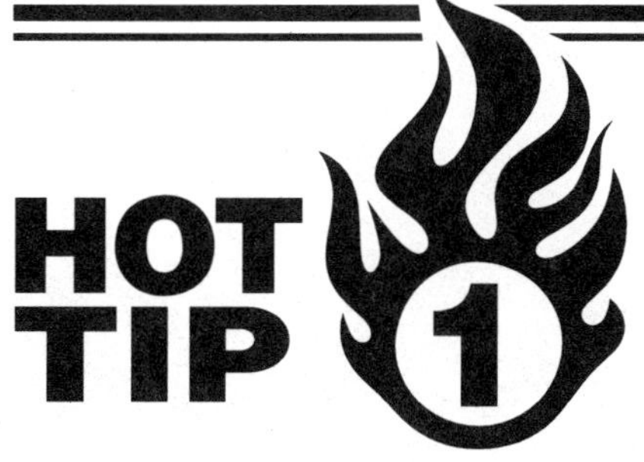

HOT TIP 1 Use Your Brain!

Find An Illustration

Get your event promotion off to a great start by combining fun and wacky art with a catchy, attention-grabbing headline. First, look through this book for a dynamic illustration that's relevant to your purpose or event. Then brainstorm for a creative headline.

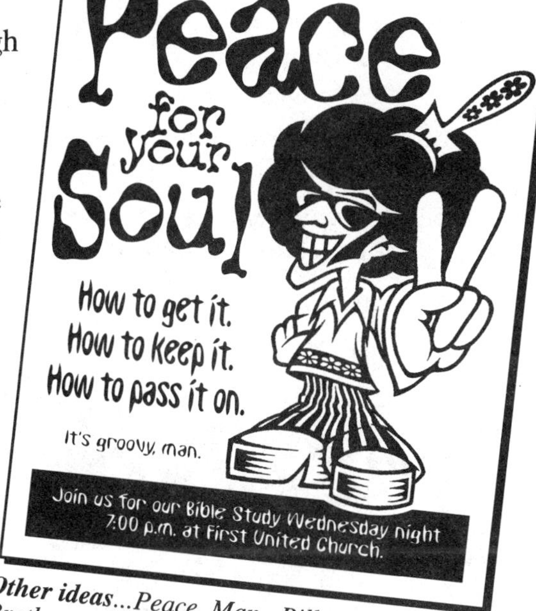

Other ideas...Peace, Man...Rilly Goovy...Soul Brother...Big Hairy Deal...Movin' & Groovin'...Jesus Freak...etc.

Make Up A Killer Headline

In the brainstorming process look for humor, shock value, or unique phrases that stick in your mind. Quickly write down all the obvious ideas and phrases that relate to the illustration. Look for plays on words, double meanings, and quirky phrases that enhance the word picture you are creating. At this point don't even try to decide if it's a good or bad idea. Get input from several creative or crazy friends. Use the dictionary, thesaurus, or slang dictionary to find additional words and phrases. Also allow enough time for your subconscious to work. Take a break and do a little daydreaming or sleep on it. Eventually one headline will probably rise to the top of the list. You may like the headline you develop so well that you'll decide to use it for the actual name of the event.

Example

NEED A GOOD SLAP?
Itchin' for a little hockey?
Join us for the game.
Fri. January 3
meet at the chuch at 6:00 p.m.
face off at 7:00

Other ideas...Power Play...Skate Date...Deep Freeze...Power & Glory...Frozen Inferno...etc.

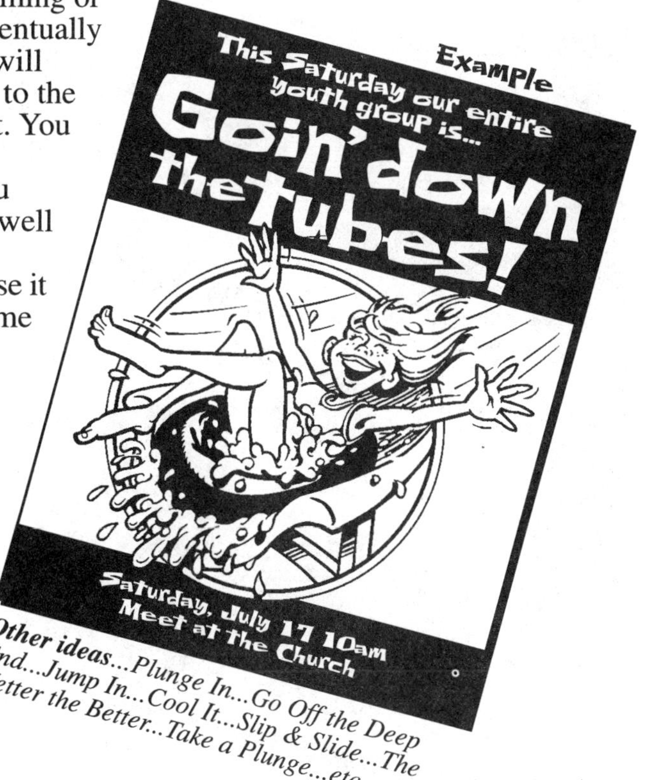

Other ideas...Plunge In...Go Off the Deep End...Jump In...Cool It...Slip & Slide...The Wetter the Better...Take a Plunge...etc.

Tie It All Together

The next step is to tie the headline and illustration to the rest of your informational copy. This may be a no-brainer if the headline is an event name and the copy is giving the important details of that event. It may be more challenging—and more fun—if you're using an illustration and headline that are a little more remote or off-the-wall. To tie it all together, usually the *very first* sentence of the copy info is used as a bridge to connect the radical illustration and headline with the body copy.

All fonts shown in examples can be ordered from Church Art Works. See ad on page 143.

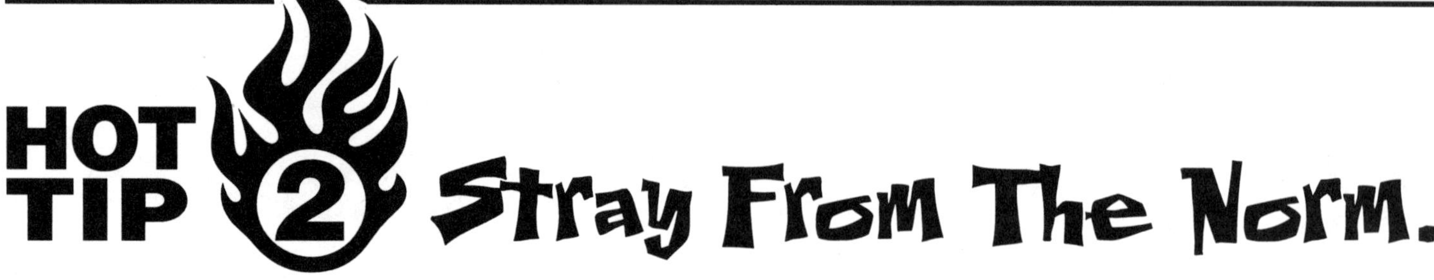

HOT TIP 2 Stray From The Norm.

Do Something Extraordinary!

Be creative in the way you use the artwork. Try the images in several different sizes and positions. Try tilting it at an angle or running it off the page. You could even use the same image more than once in the same or different sizes to create a pattern. Experimentation leads to creative solutions.

When you find the arrangement that you like best, use your type to fill in the space around the artwork. You may be surprised at all the interesting looks you can create.

Remember that you don't need to use your art exactly as it appears in this book. Don't be afraid to enlarge, crop, or combine elements, or to use only a portion of the image. **Be creative!**

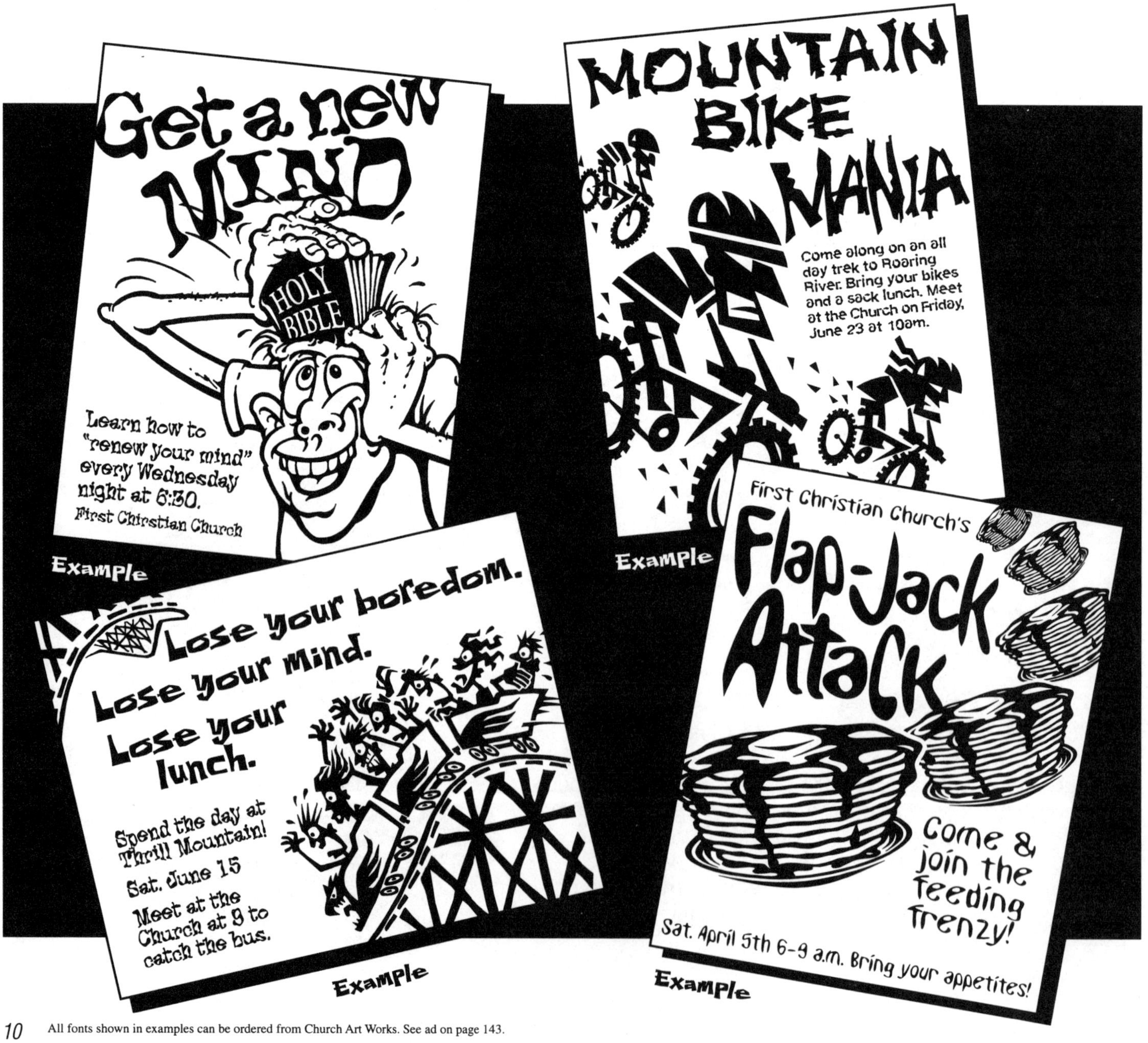

Get a new MIND

HOLY BIBLE

Learn how to "renew your mind" every Wednesday night at 6:30.
First Chirstian Church

Example

MOUNTAIN BIKE MANIA

Come along on an all day trek to Roaring River. Bring your bikes and a sack lunch. Meet at the Church on Friday, June 23 at 10am.

Example

Lose your boredom.
Lose your Mind.
Lose your lunch.

Spend the day at Thrill Mountain!
Sat. June 15
Meet at the Church at 9 to catch the bus.

Example

First Christian Church's
Flap-Jack Attack
Come & join the feeding frenzy!
Sat. April 5th 6-9 a.m. Bring your appetites!

Example

 All fonts shown in examples can be ordered from Church Art Works. See ad on page 143.

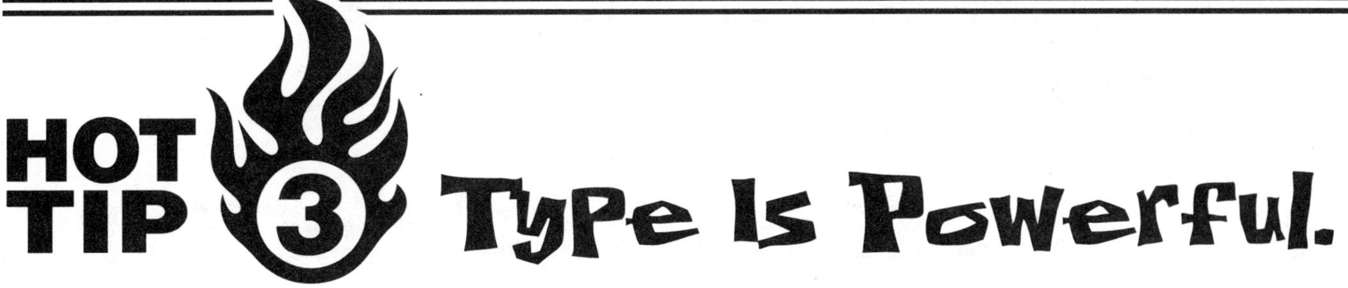

HOT TIP 3 Type Is Powerful.

Obviously, illustrations are an important part of any promotion. But did you know that the font (typeface) you choose can also have a huge impact on the final look of your piece? Pick a headline font that goes with the look of your art. If your artwork is wild and crazy, you probably need a typeface that is crazy too. If the art is more reserved, you shouldn't get too wild with your type. As a general rule, you can get almost as funky as you want for headlines, but you should use a more readable style for your general information type.

If you have a computer you may want to invest in some wacky fonts (like the One Way Out® fonts on page 143). If you don't have a computer or don't have the budget to buy fonts, there are a few things you can do to spice up the type you have access to.

With kickin' fonts (Sweet!)

With plain fonts (Lame)

Print out a bold typeface (or have someone print it out for you). Use the copier to enlarge and reduce the words in different sizes. Cut and paste the letters onto a paper, using various sizes of letters (similar to a ransom note). You can tilt some of the letters and overlap them to get an interesting, haphazard look.You can even take it a step further and thrash the letters by cutting them in half or cutting pieces off them and gluing them back on imperfectly so you end up with overlapping in some places and white crevices in others. Also, you can take Scotch tape and wrap it around your finger and lightly touch the black areas to pull up some of the toner in a random fashion. You can go as far as you want–but keep in mind that you want to be able to *read* the final product.When you get what you like, make a new copy so you will have a nice clean headline to combine with your art.

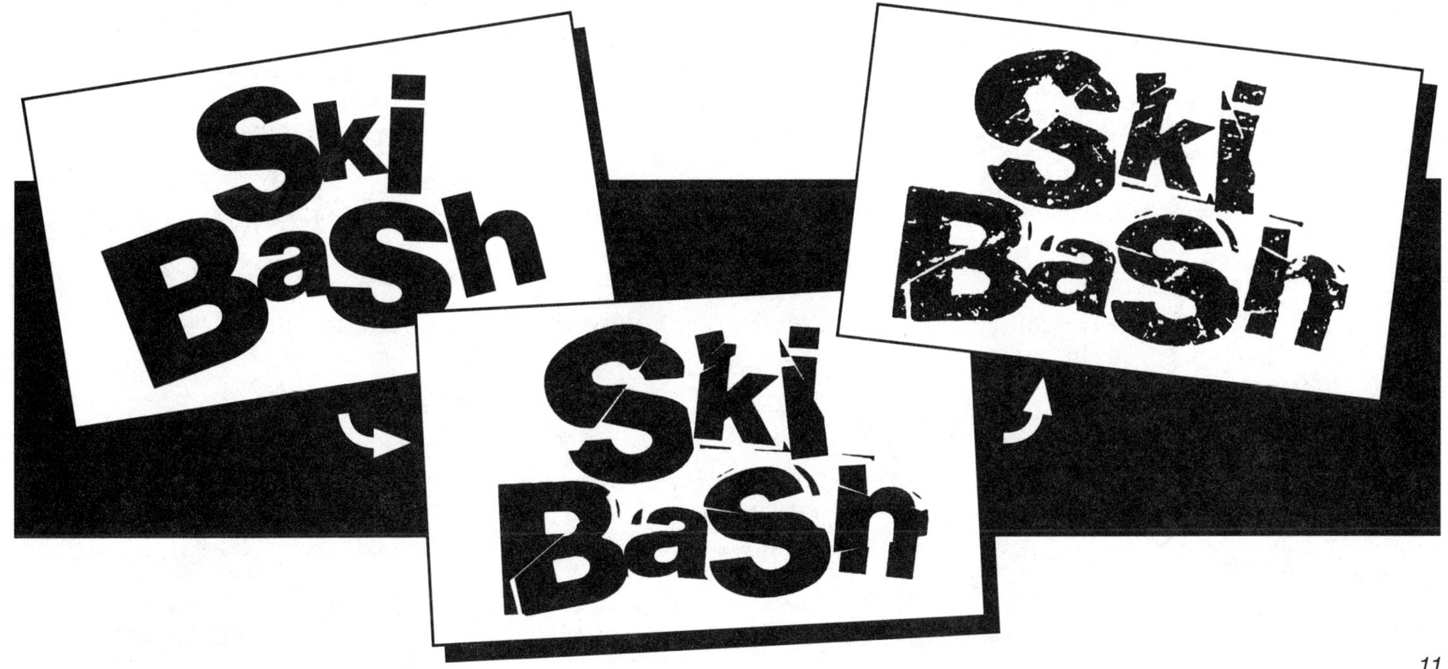

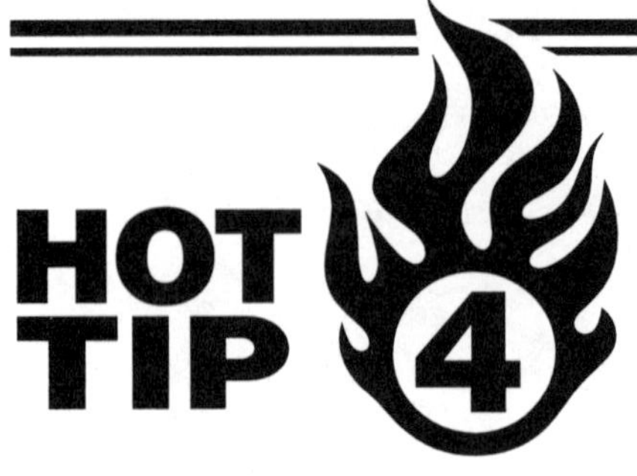

Expand Your Horizons.

Variety Is Your Friend!

As you are looking through this resource be thinking of ways to use the art. Here are some examples to start with.

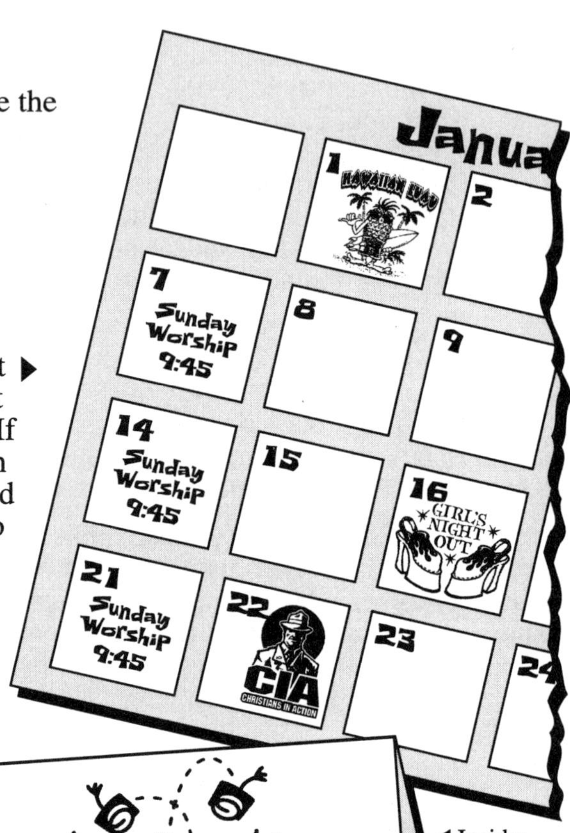

◀ ***Fliers*** are an inexpensive way to get the word out. They're powerful, and they're quick!

Calendars are a great ▶ place to drop in art that relates to your events. If you use the same art on your fliers, posters, and whatever else relates to your event, your promotions will have continuity. That's a *good* thing!

Inside: ▶
Date:
Time:
Place:
From:

Make funny ***greeting cards*** that kids respond to. Keep three or four different designs on hand so that you'll have cards to send for a variety of purposes ◀ like birthdays, ▶ invitations, encouragement, missed you, etc.

◀ Inside:
It's nice to know that miracles still happen.

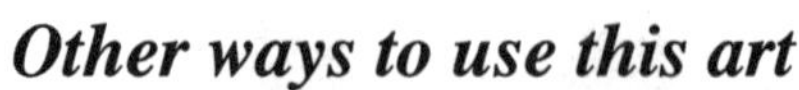

Other ways to use this art

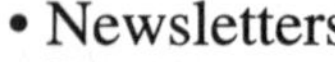

- Newsletters
- Posters
- Brochures
- Buttons
- Notepaper
- Event tickets
- Bookmarks
- Banners
- Web sites
- Powerpoint presentations

There's *no end* to the possibilities!

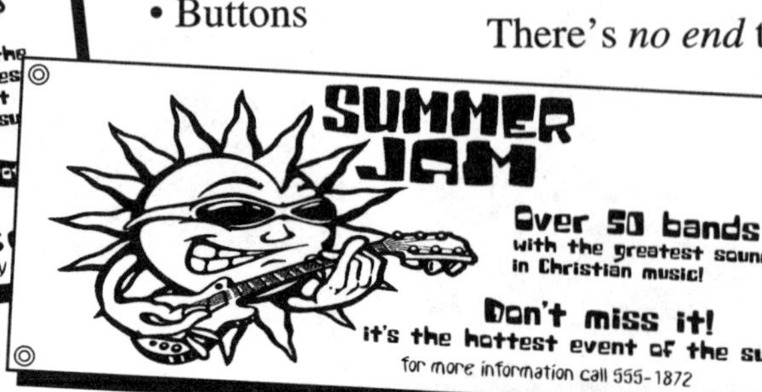

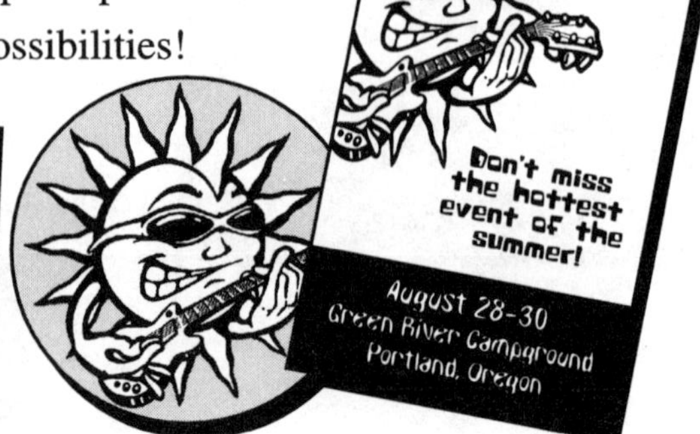

Now go forth & create!

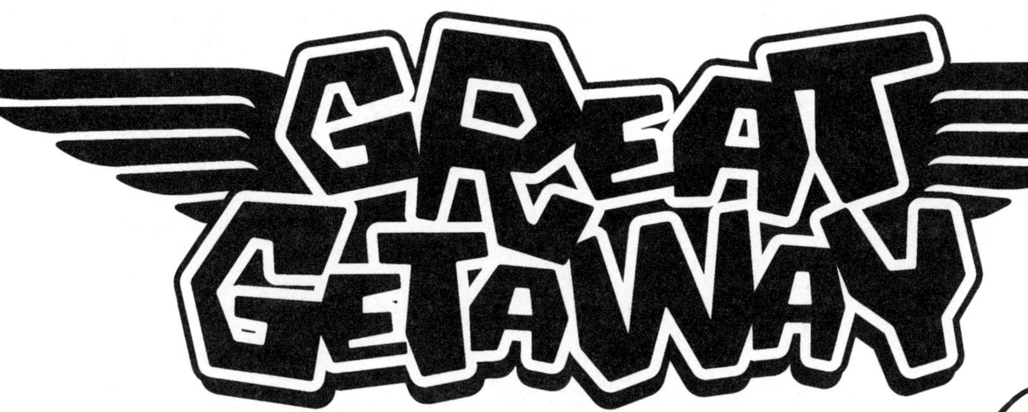
GREAT
GETAWAY

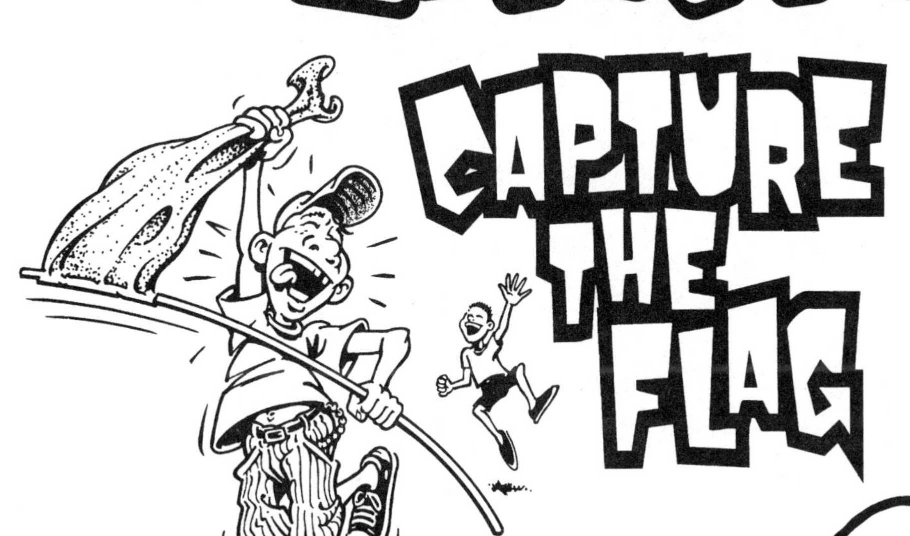
CAPTURE
THE
FLAG

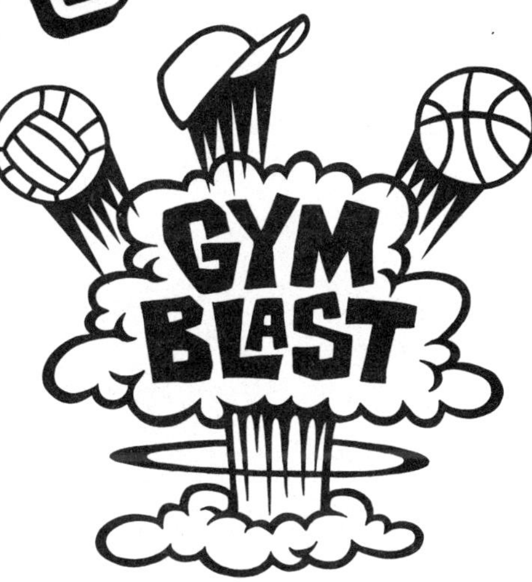
GYM
BLAST

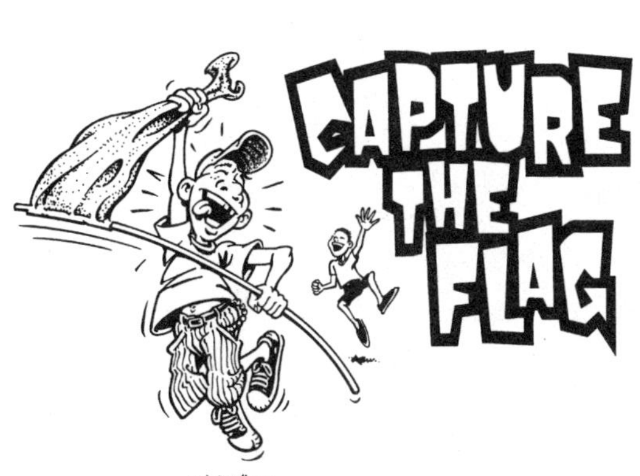
CAPTURE
THE
FLAG

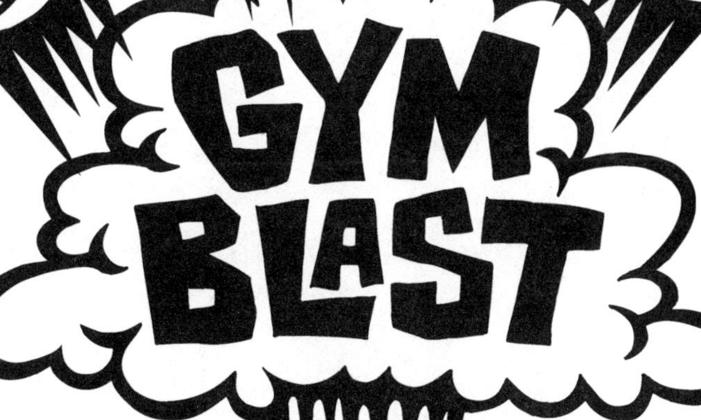
GYM
BLAST

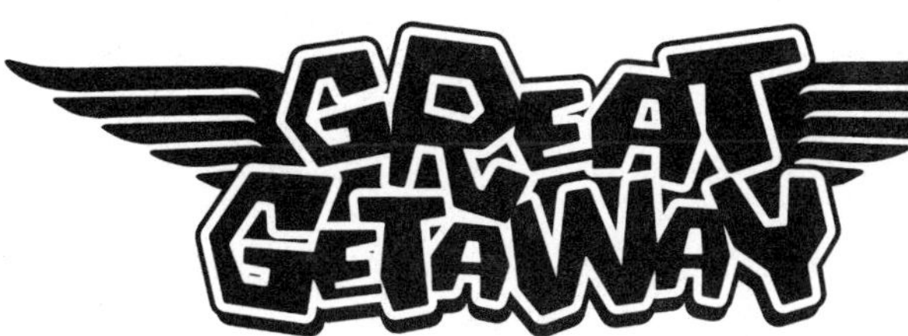
GREAT
GETAWAY

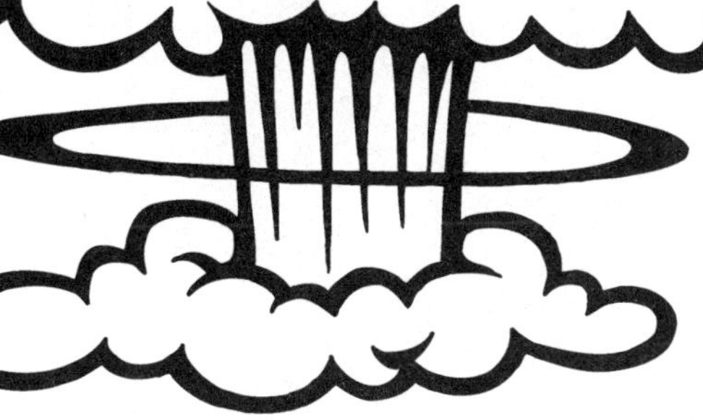

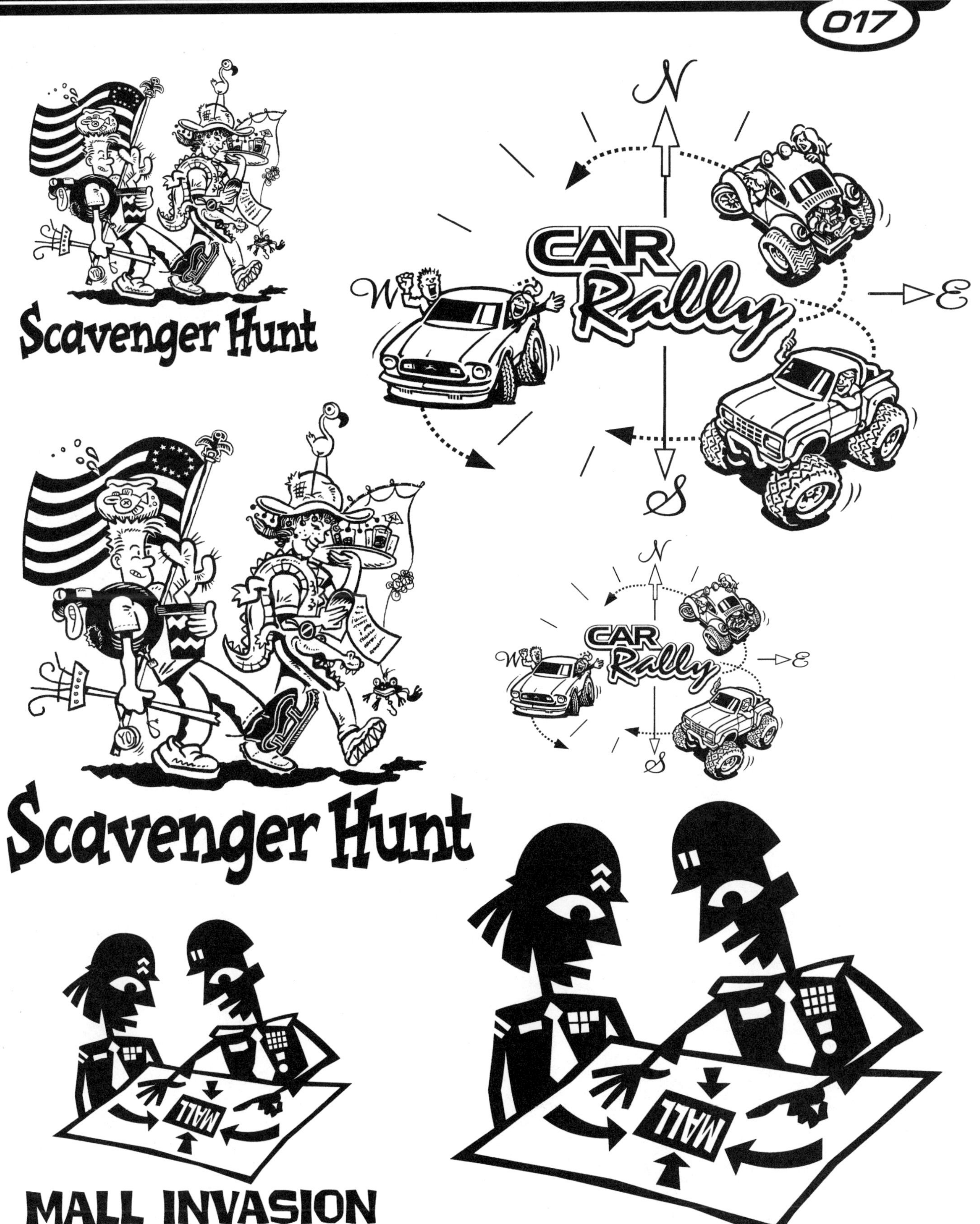
Scavenger Hunt
N
CAR Rally
W
E
S
Scavenger Hunt
N
CAR Rally
W
E
S
MALL
MALL INVASION
MALL
MALL INVASION

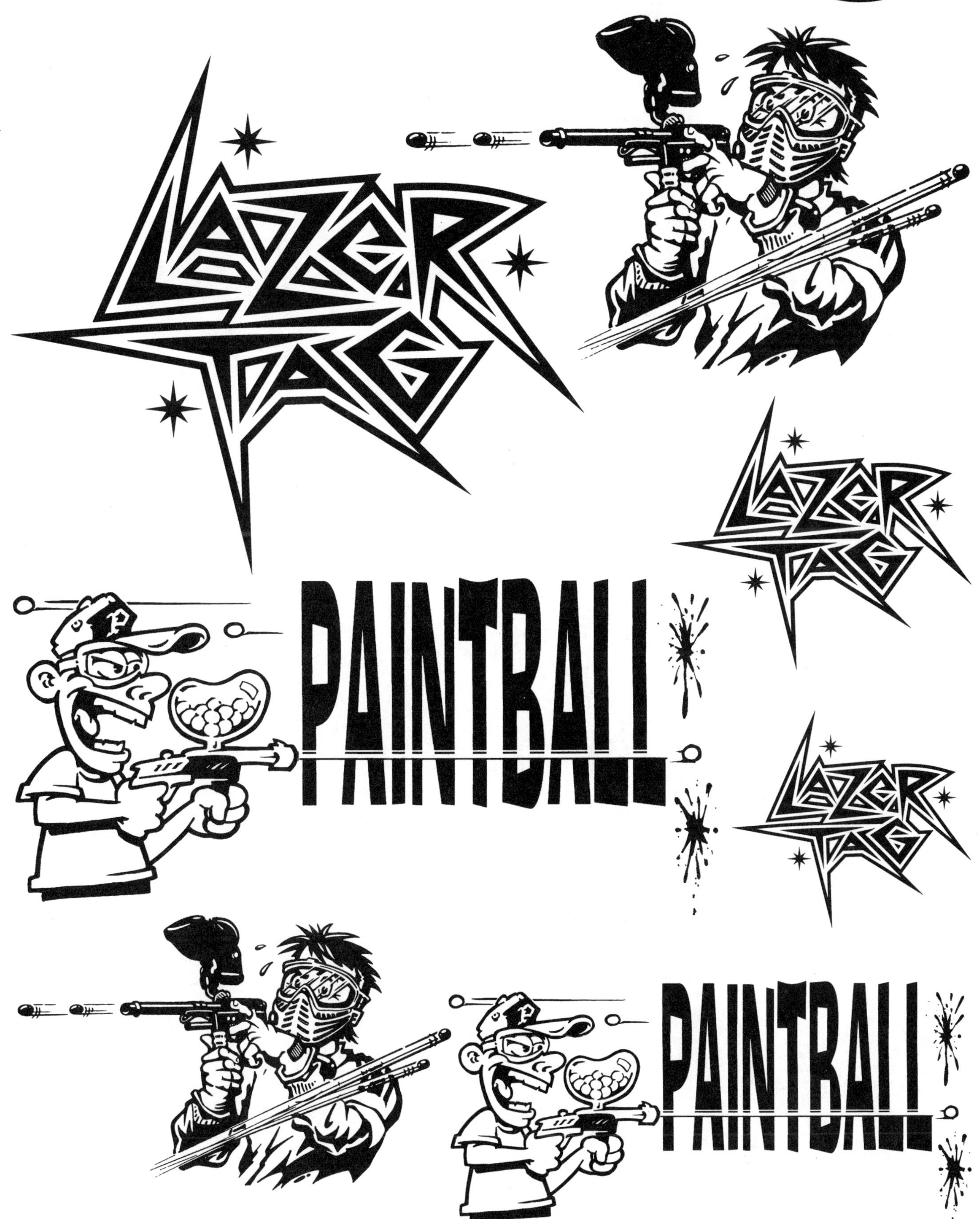
LAZER TAG
PAINTBALL
LAZER TAG
LAZER TAG
PAINTBALL

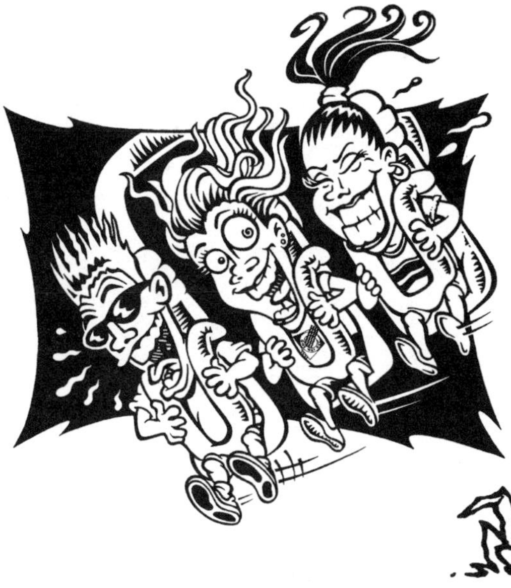

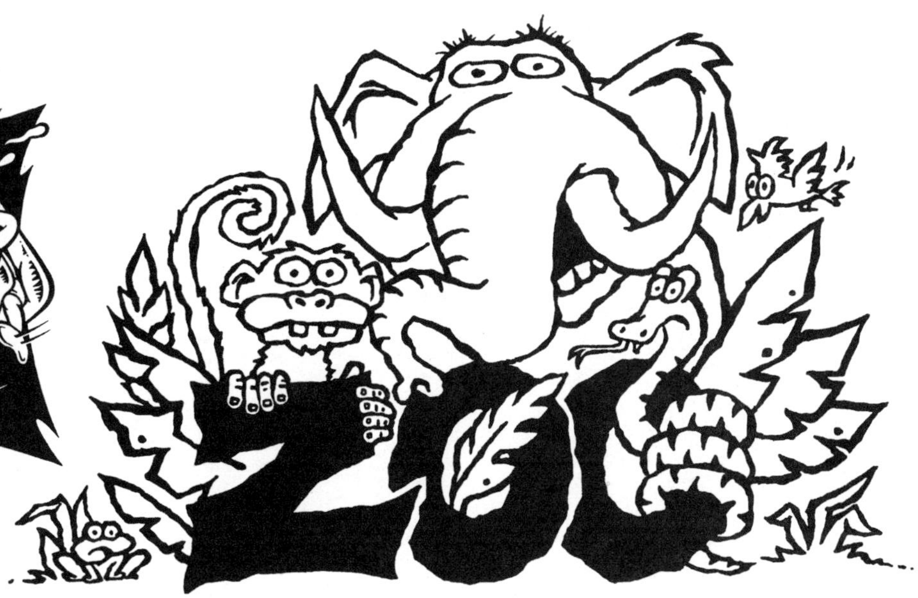

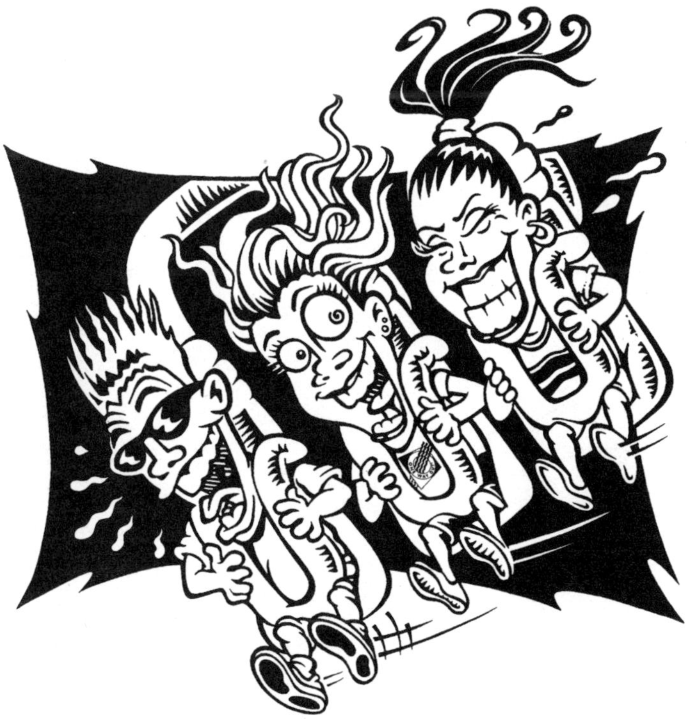

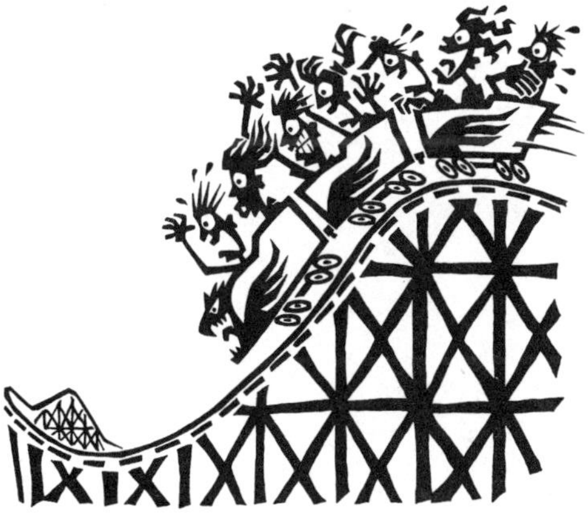

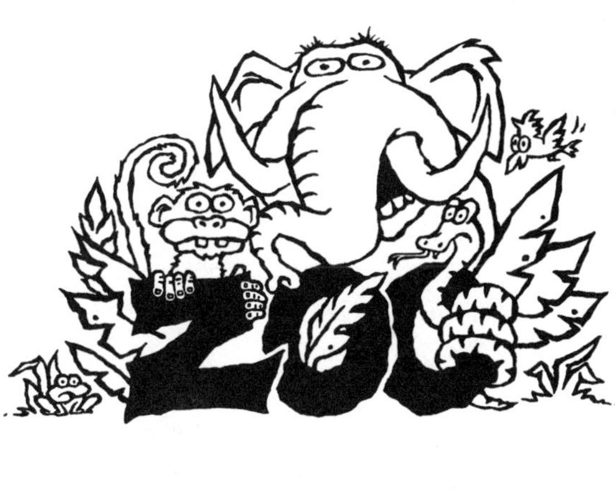

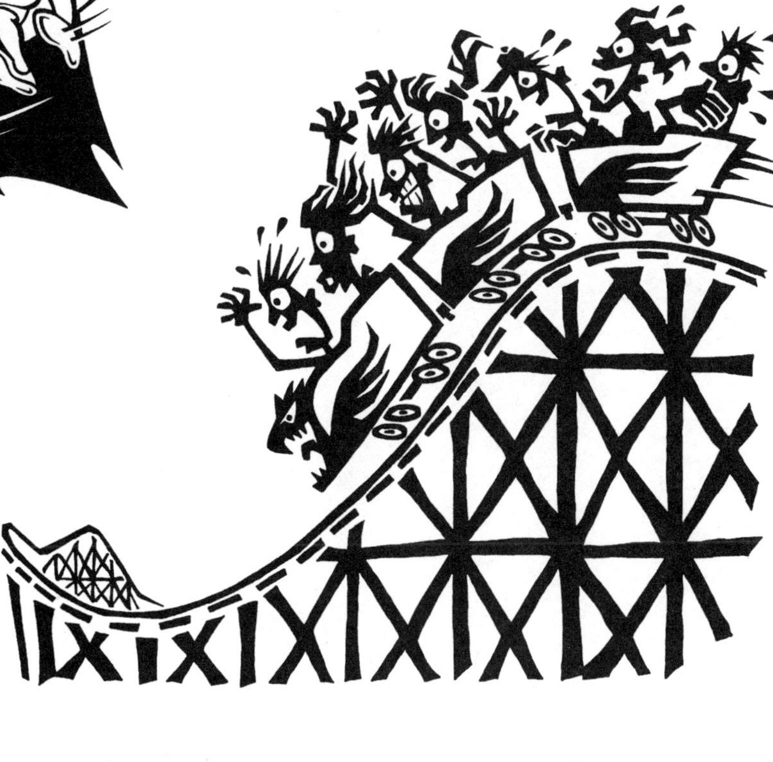

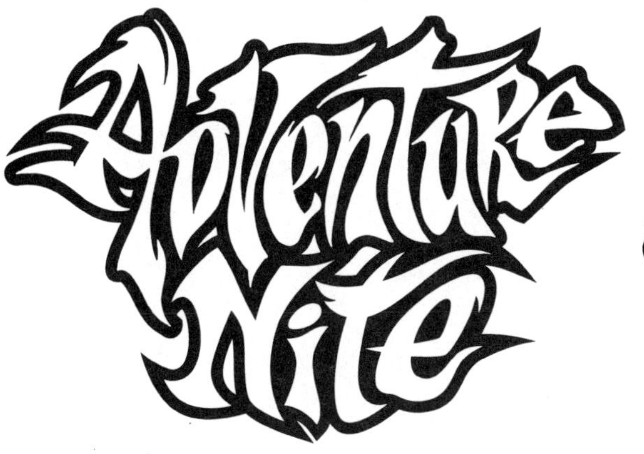
Adventure
Nite

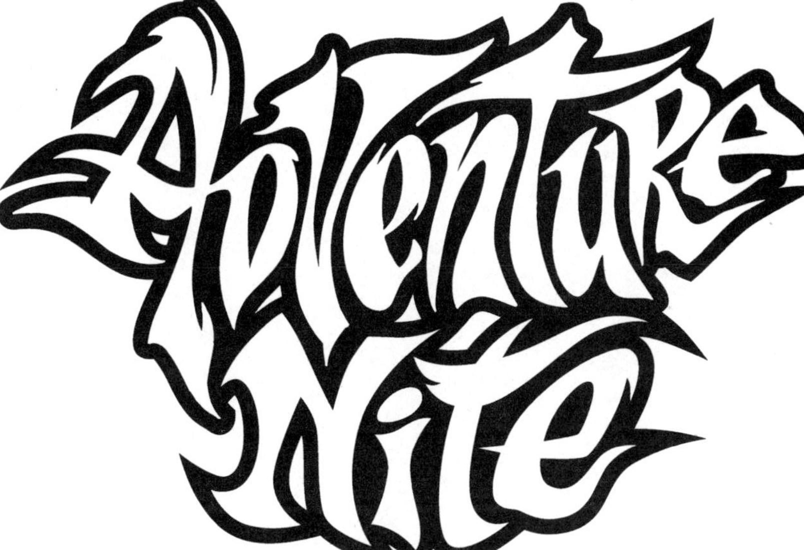
Adventure
Nite

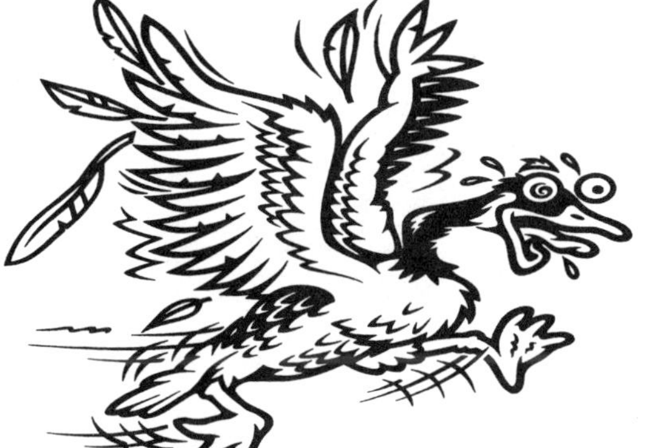

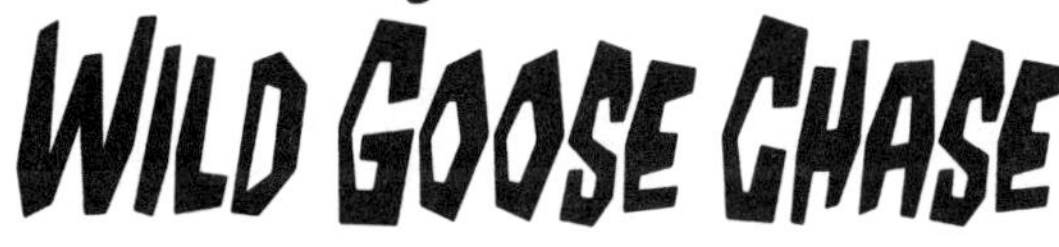
WILD GOOSE CHASE

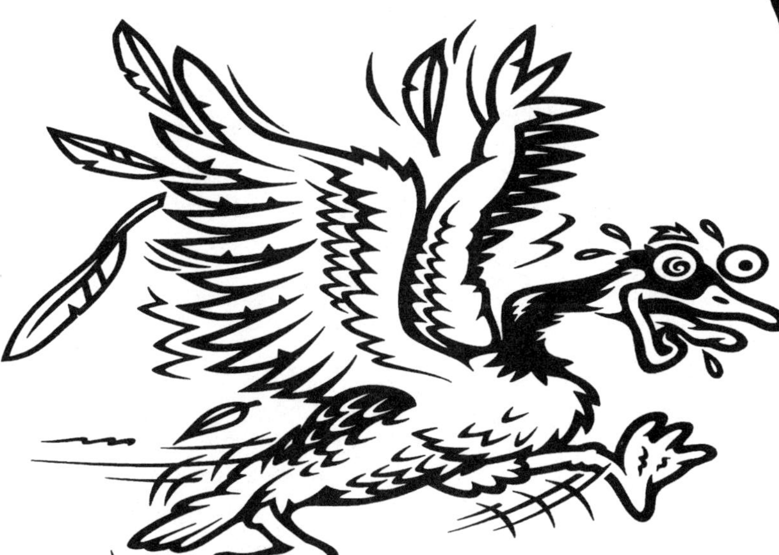
WILD GOOSE CHASE

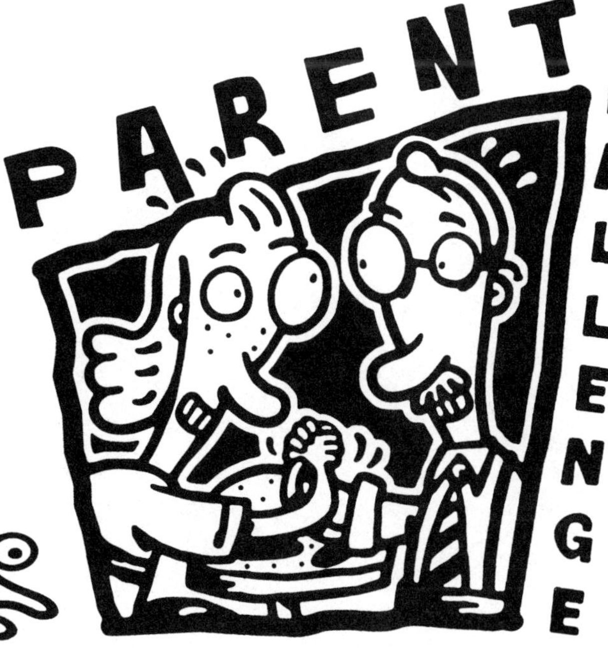
PARENT
CHALLENGE

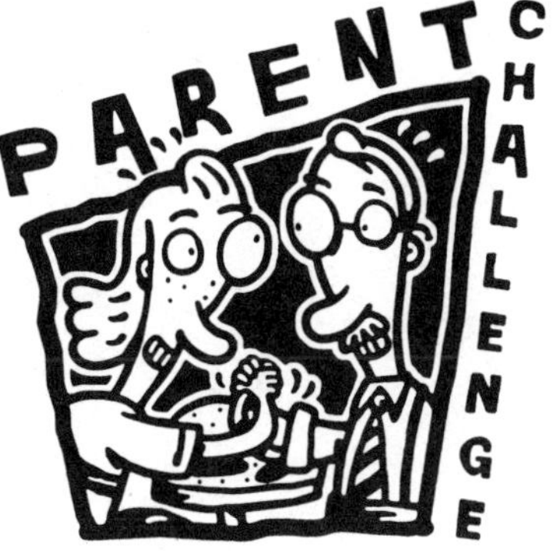
PARENT
CHALLENGE

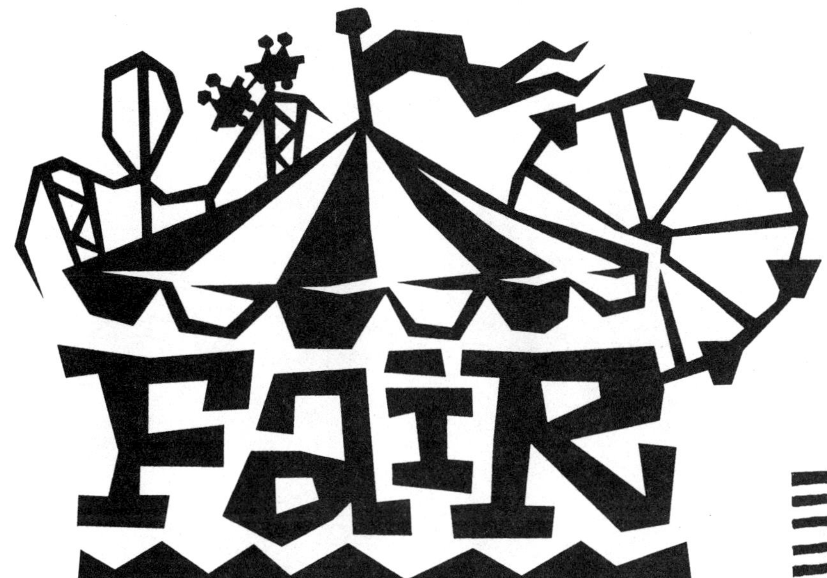
FAIR

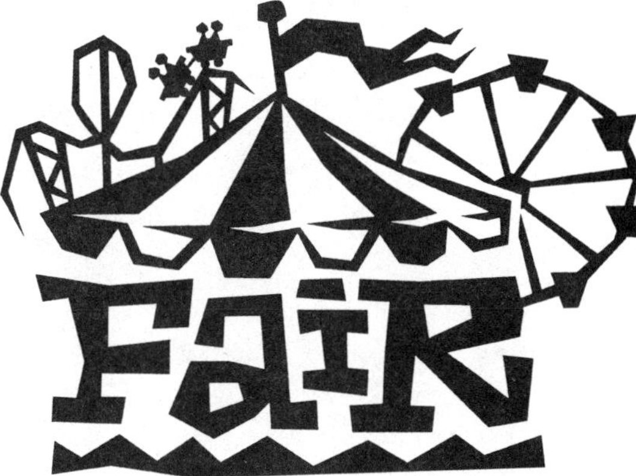
FAIR

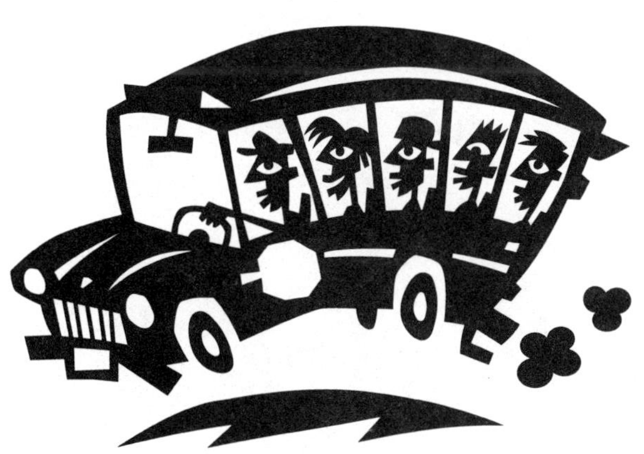

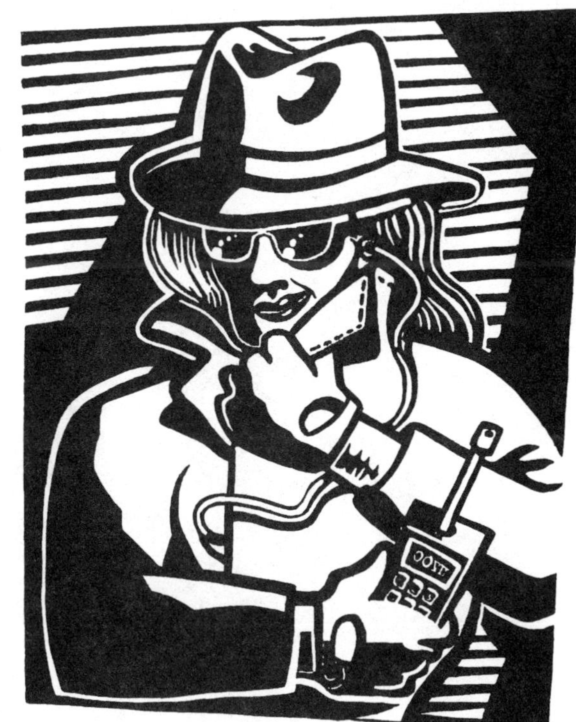

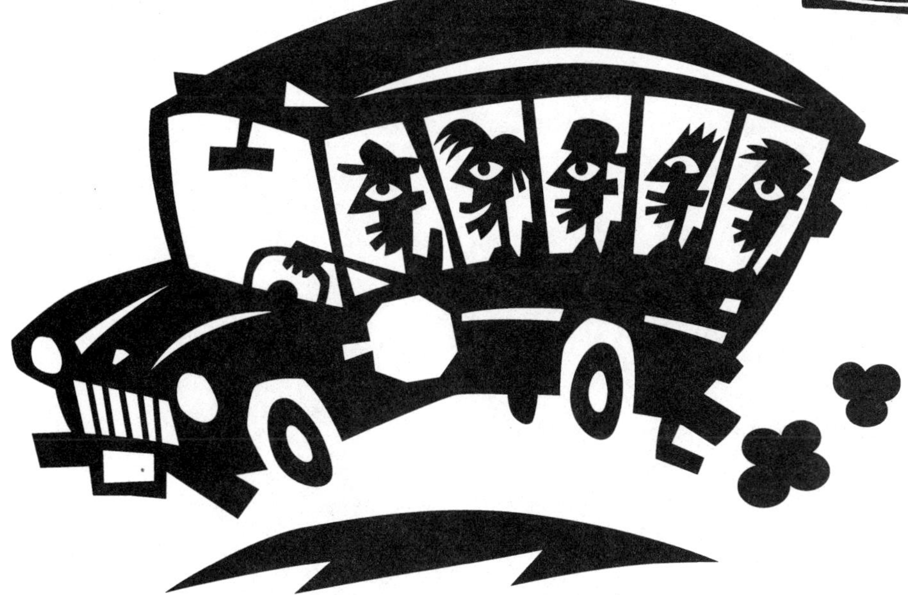

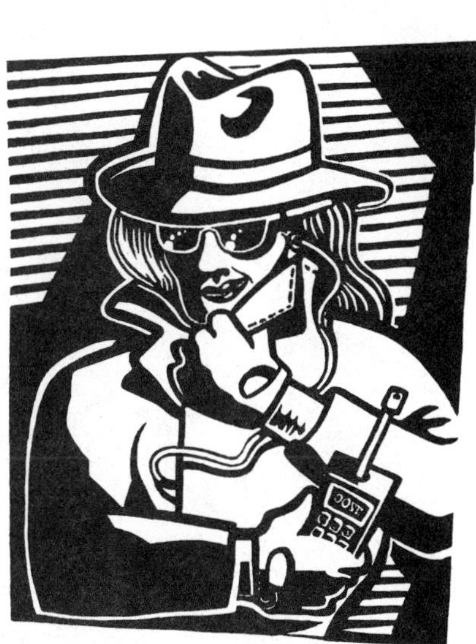

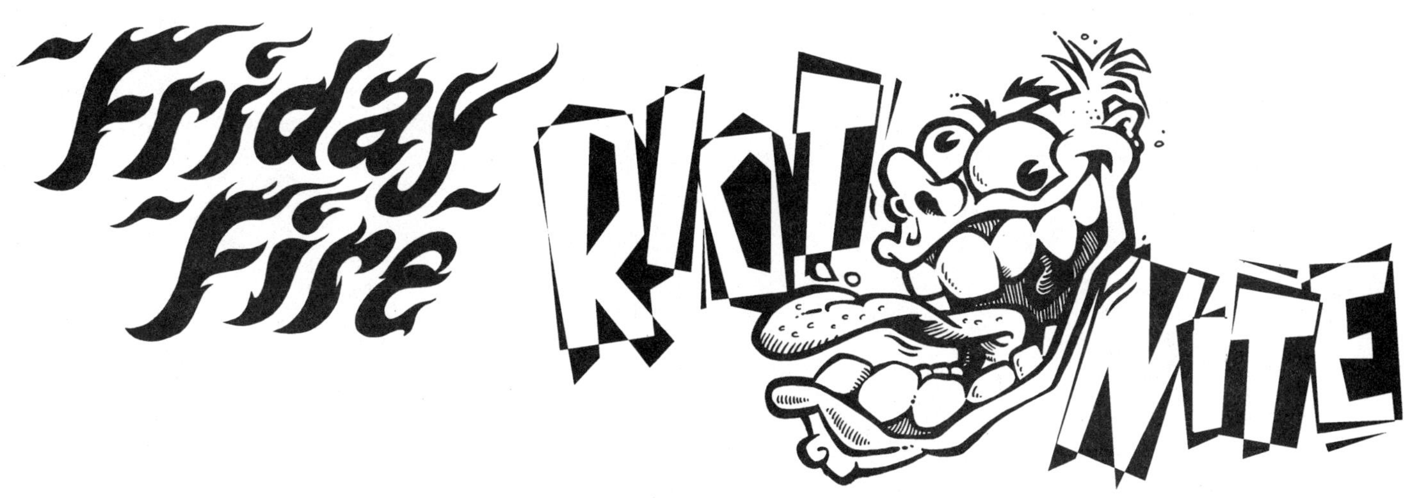

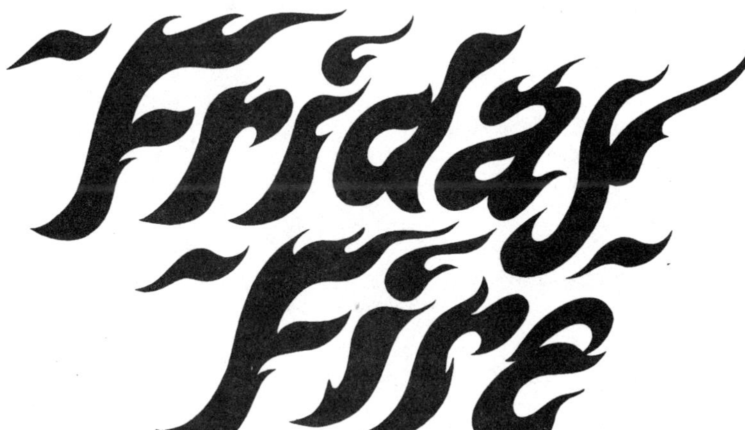

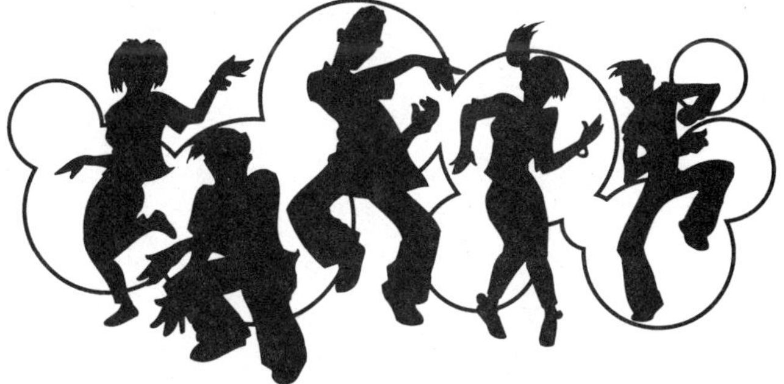

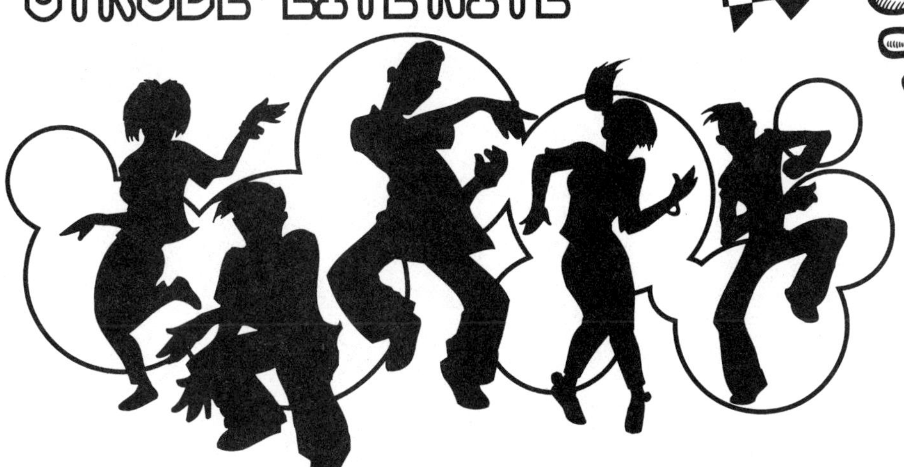

RIOT NITE

Friday Fire

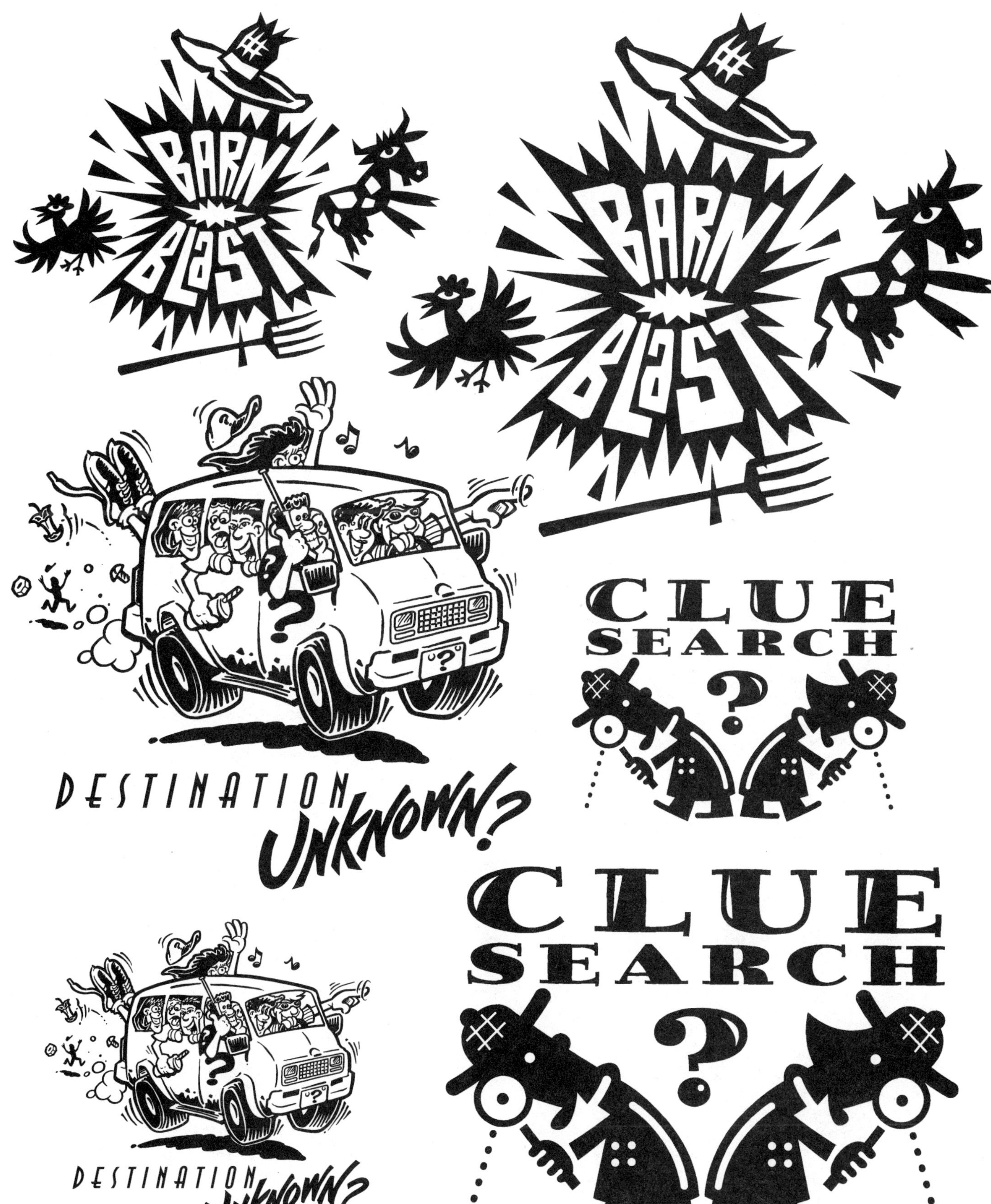
BARN BLAST
BARN BLAST
DESTINATION UNKNOWN?
CLUE SEARCH
?
CLUE SEARCH
?
DESTINATION UNKNOWN?

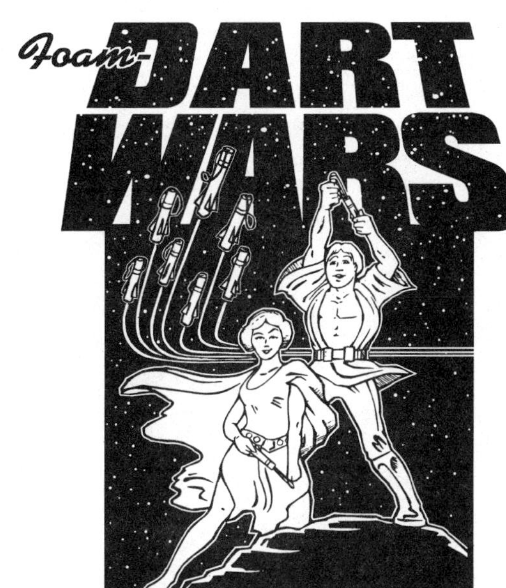

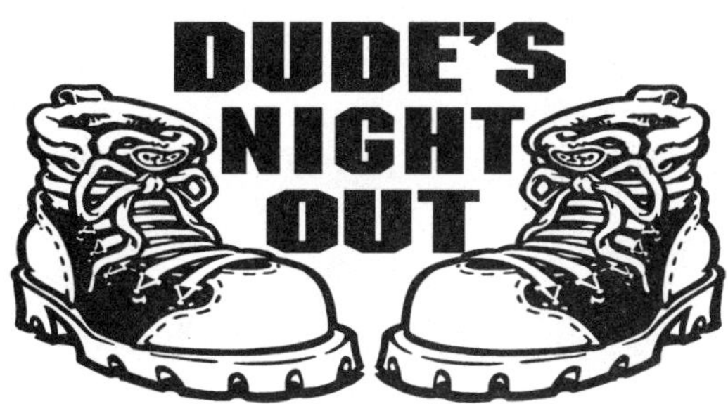

Foam-
DART
WARS

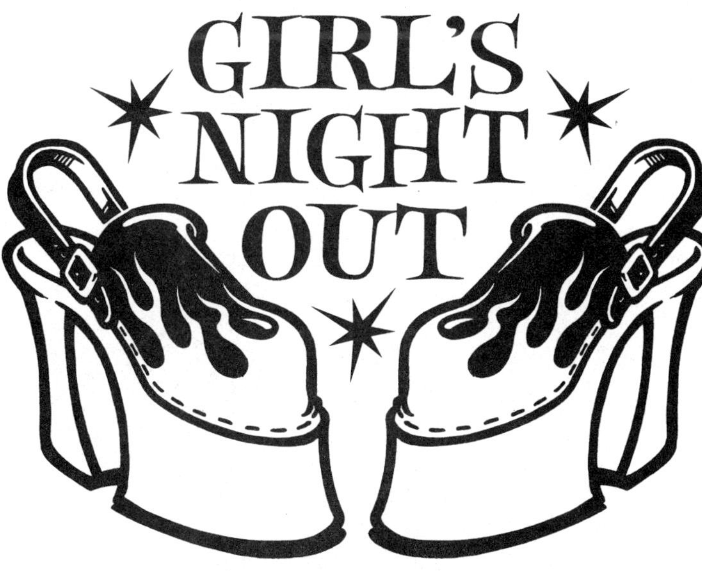

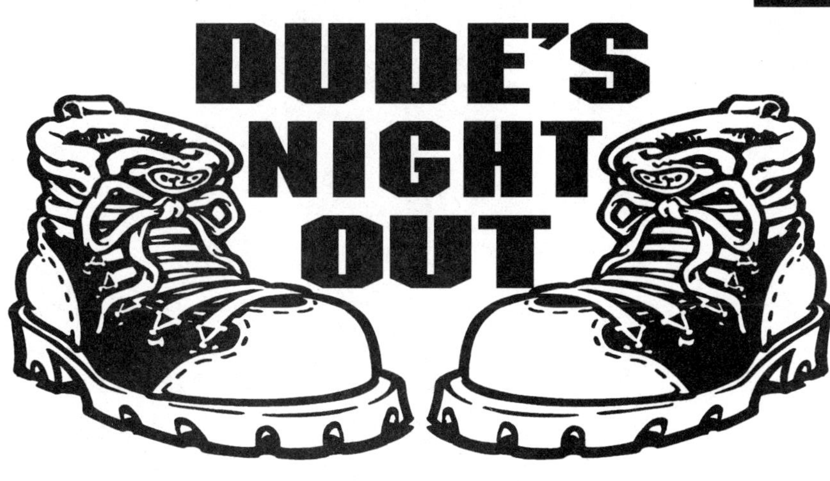

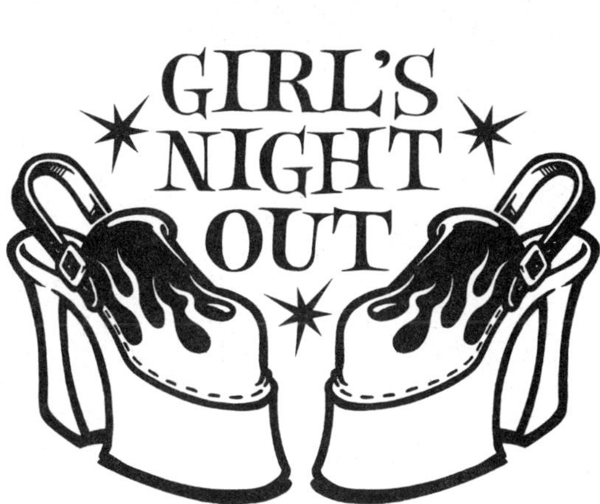

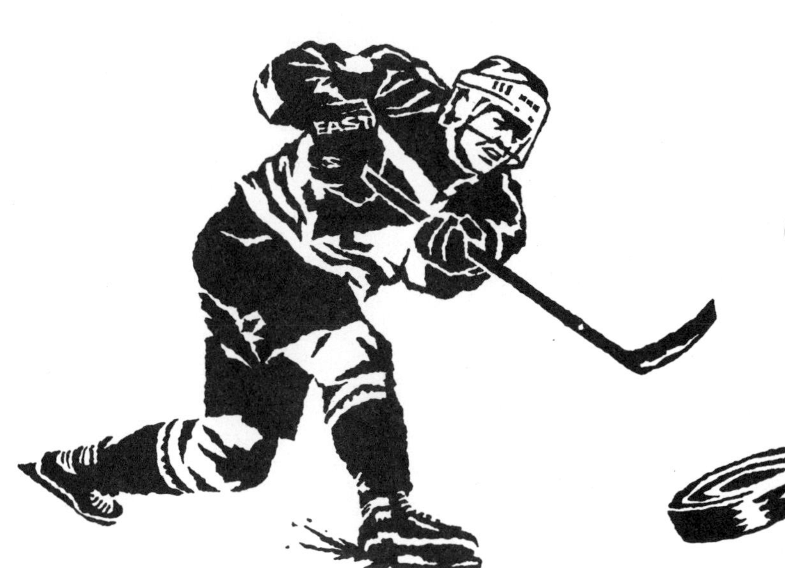

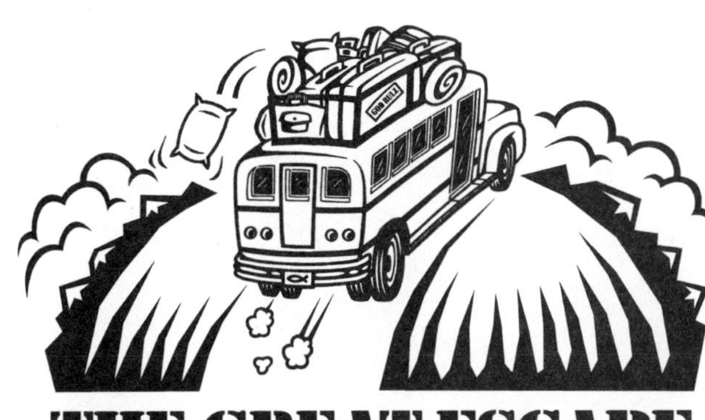

THE GREAT ESCAPE

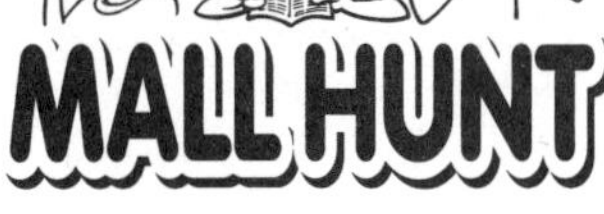

MALL HUNT

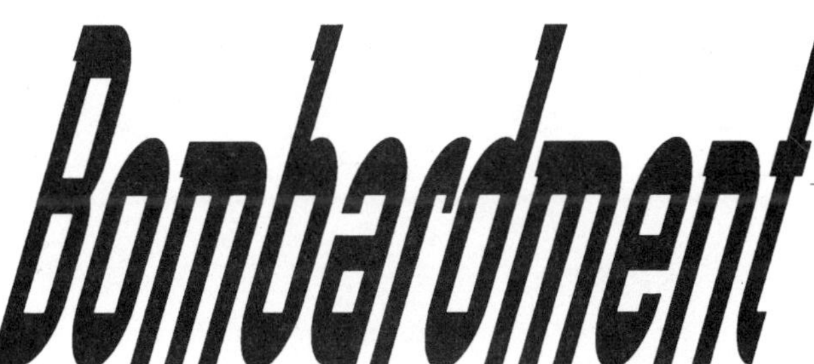

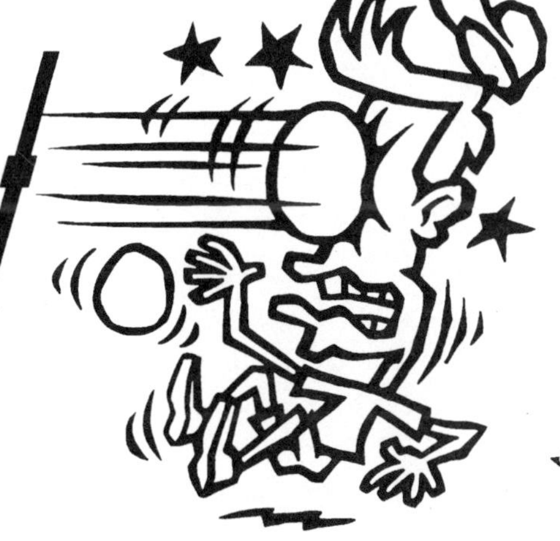

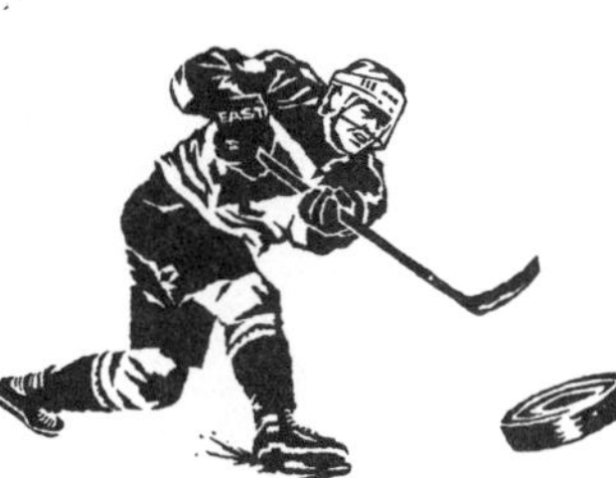

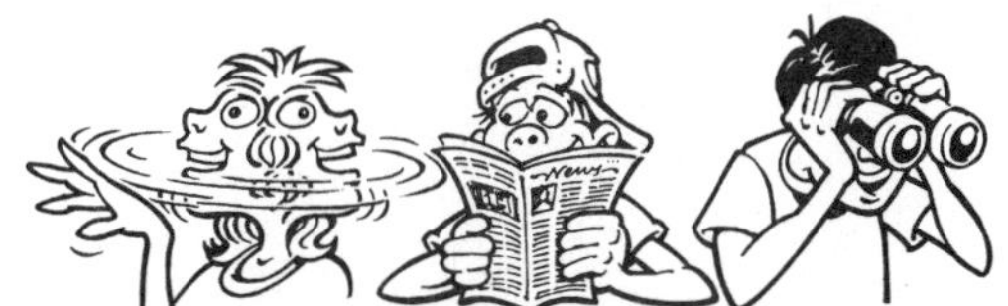

MALL HUNT

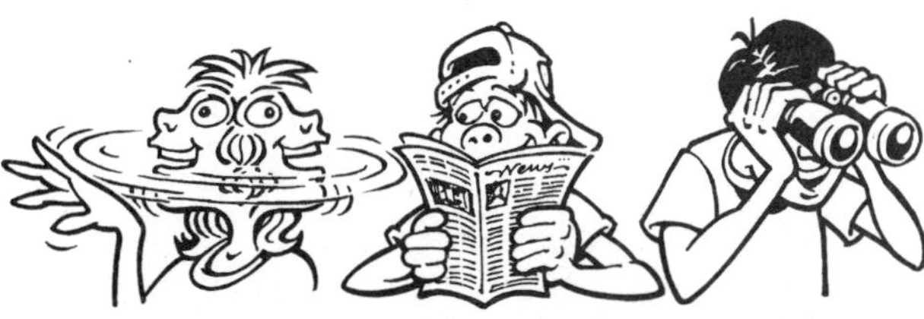

MALL HUNT

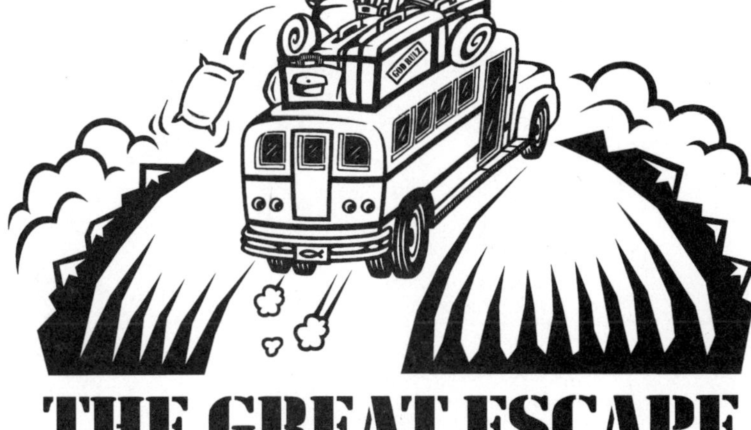

THE GREAT ESCAPE

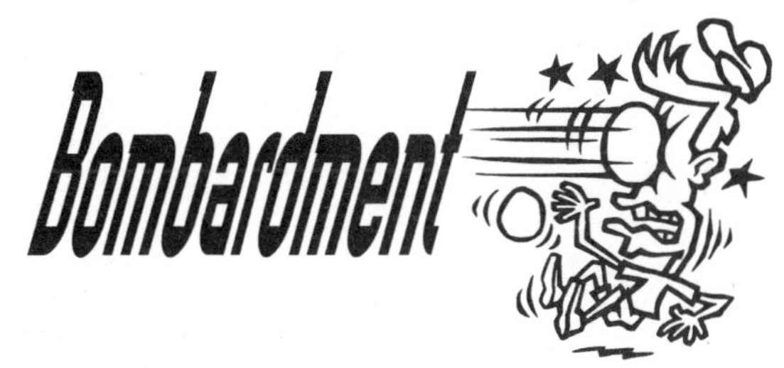

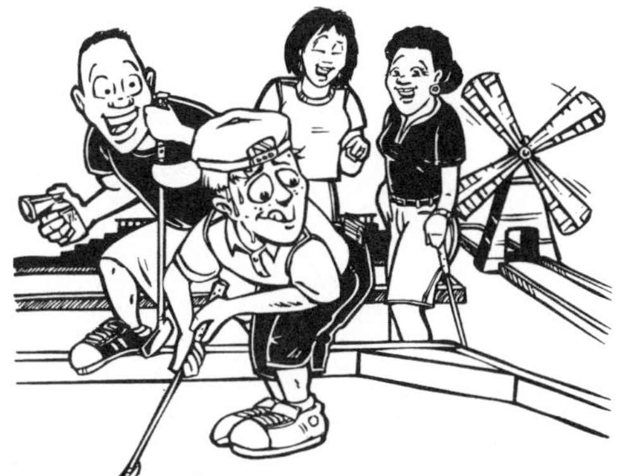
Miniature Golf

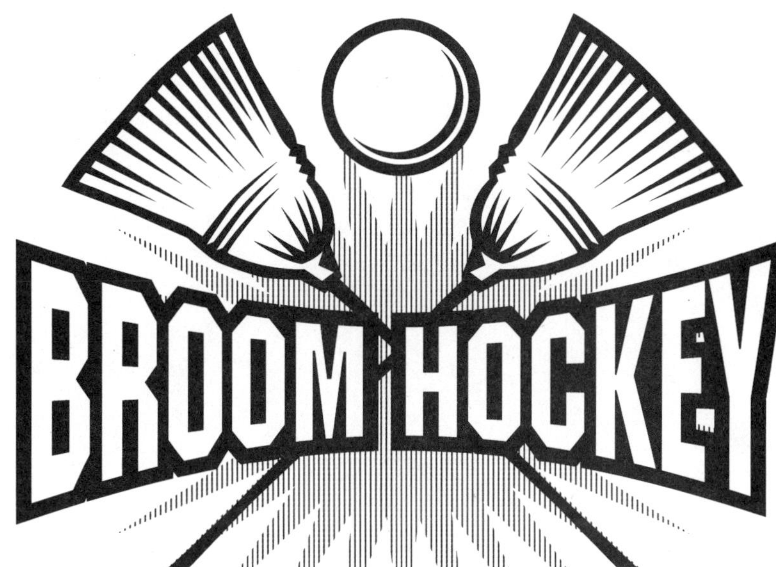
BROOM HOCKEY

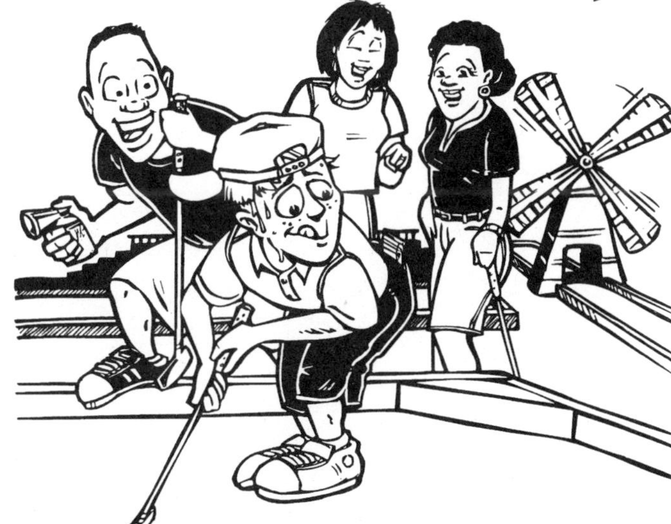
Miniature Golf

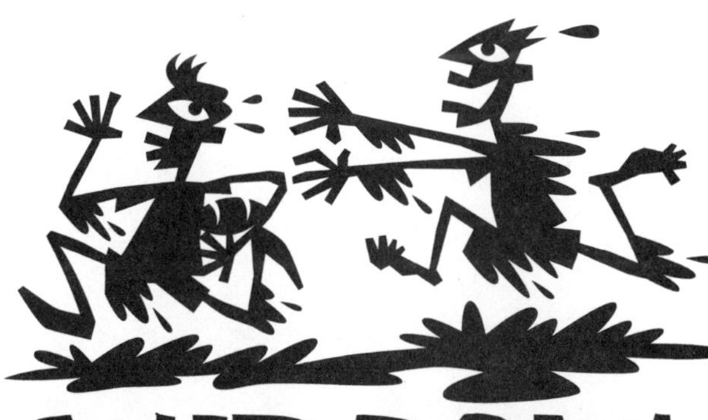
MUD BOWL

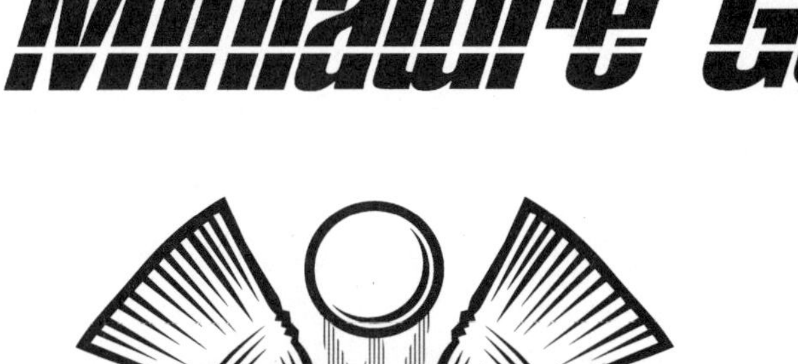

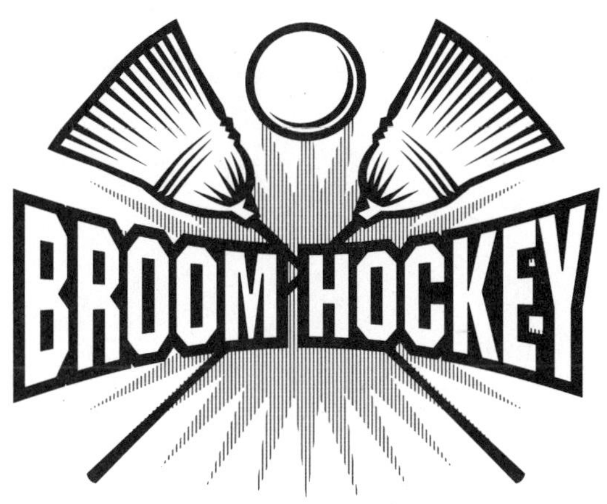
BROOM HOCKEY

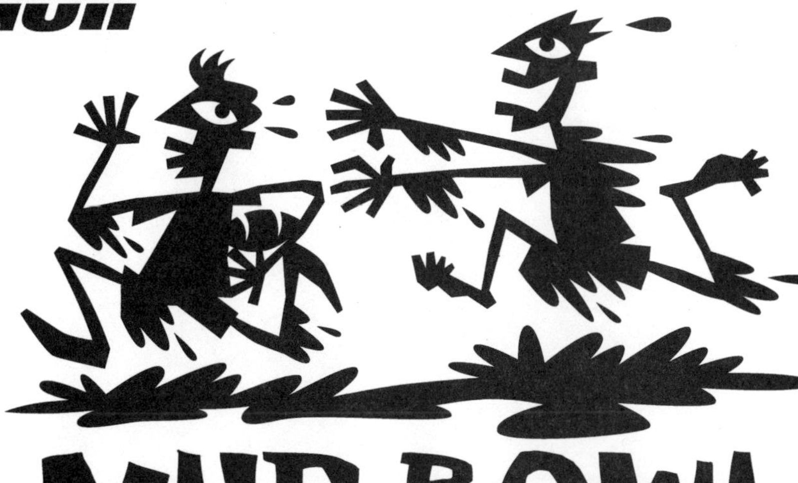
MUD BOWL

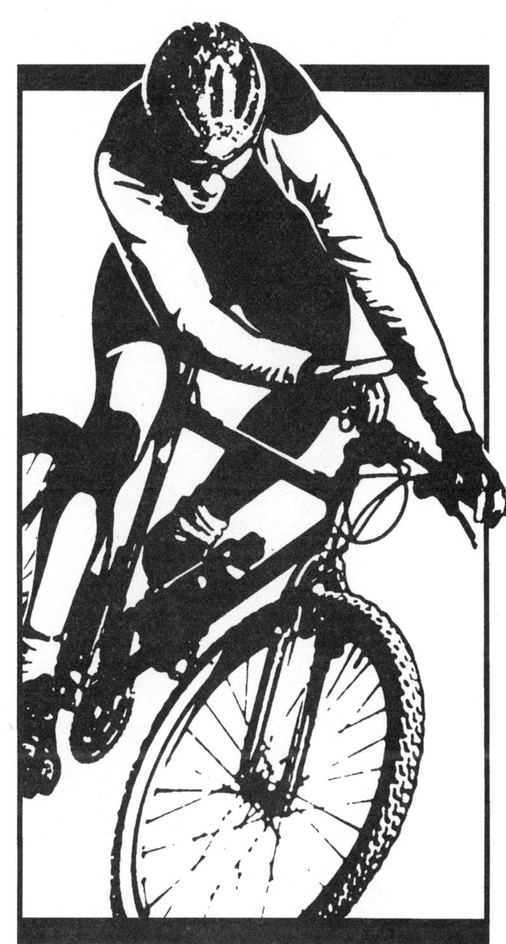

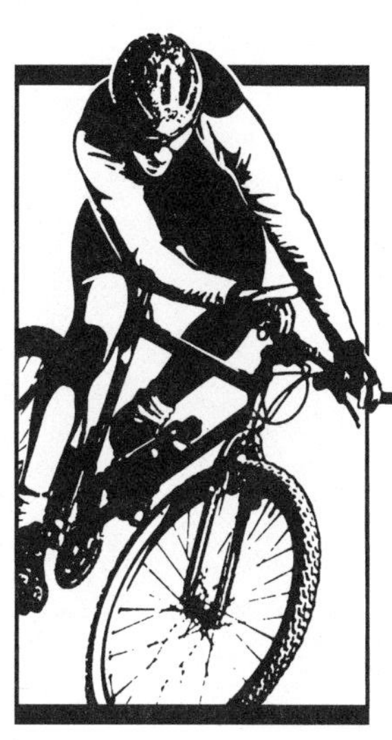

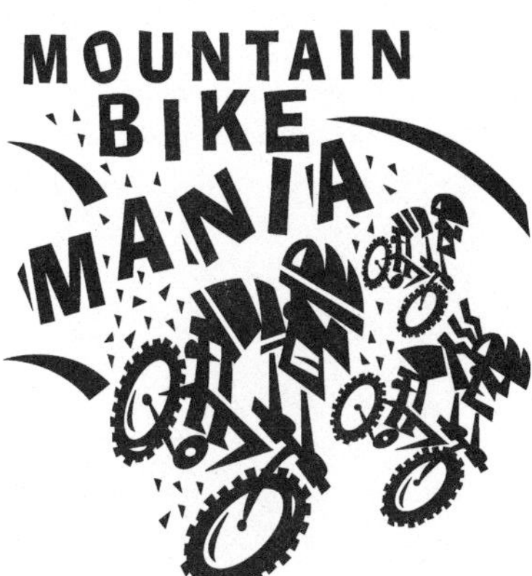

going to
Xtremes

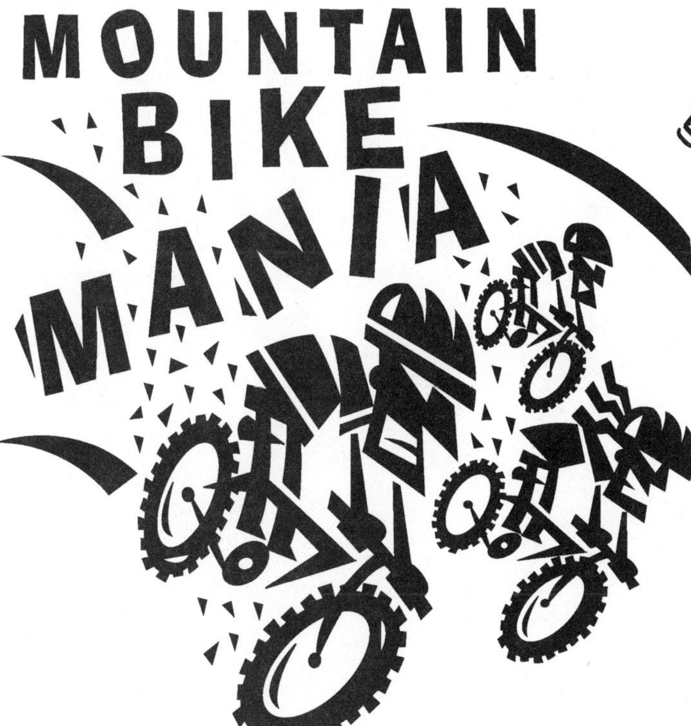

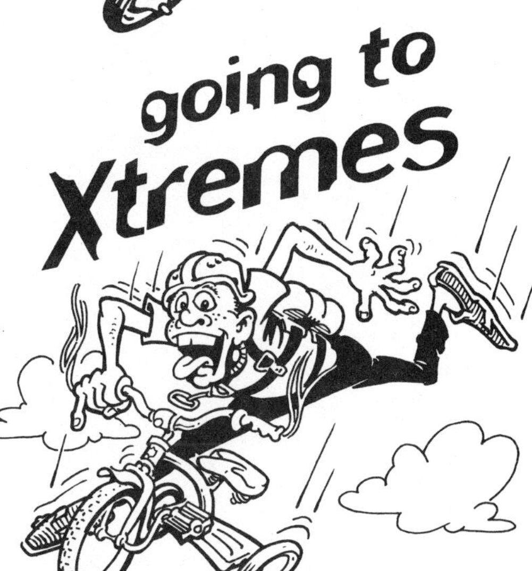

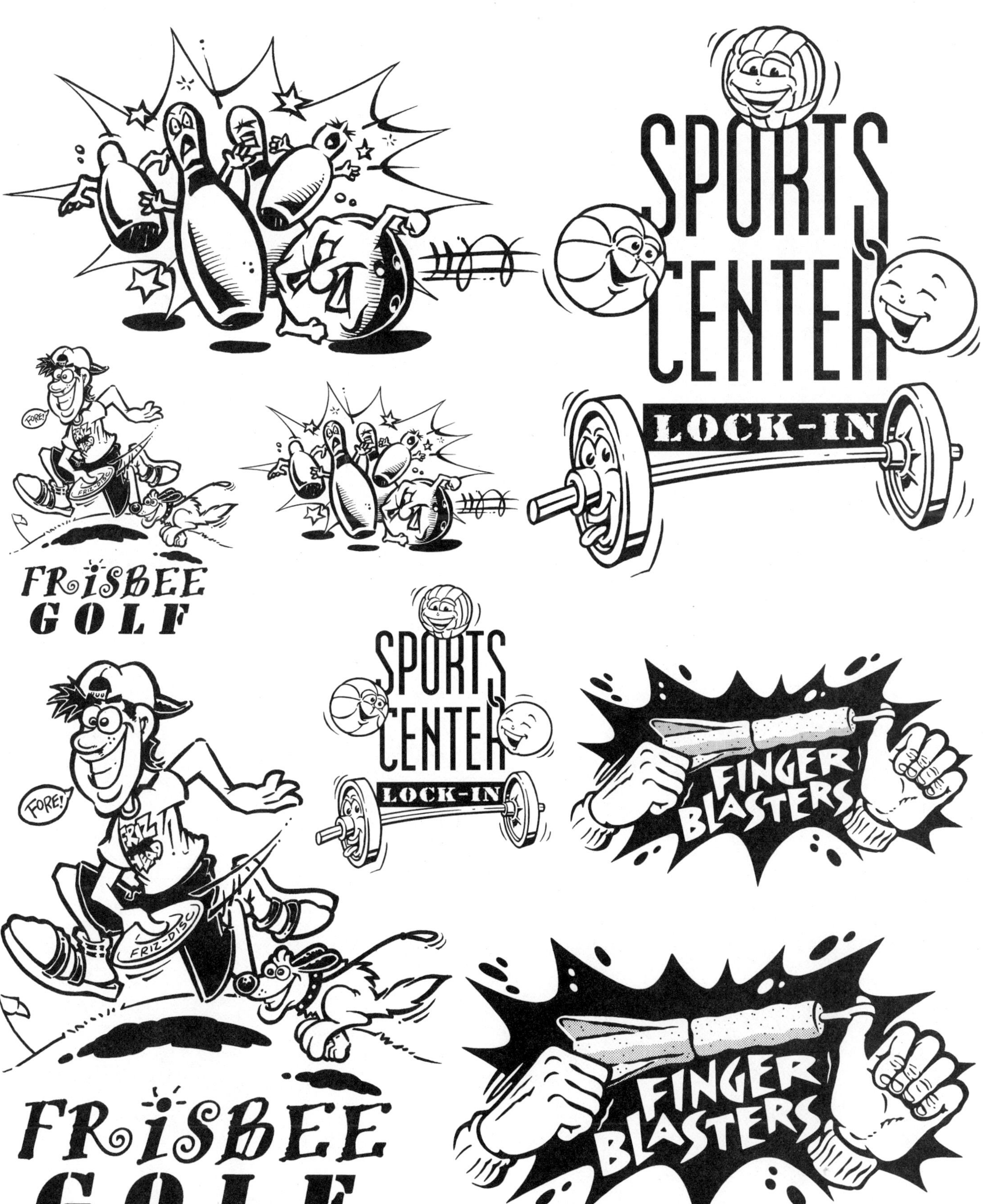
SPORTS CENTER
LOCK-IN
FORE!
FRIZ HEAD
FRIZ-DISC
FRISBEE GOLF
SPORTS CENTER
LOCK-IN
FINGER BLASTERS
FORE!
FRIZ HEAD
FRIZ-DISC
FINGER BLASTERS
FRISBEE GOLF

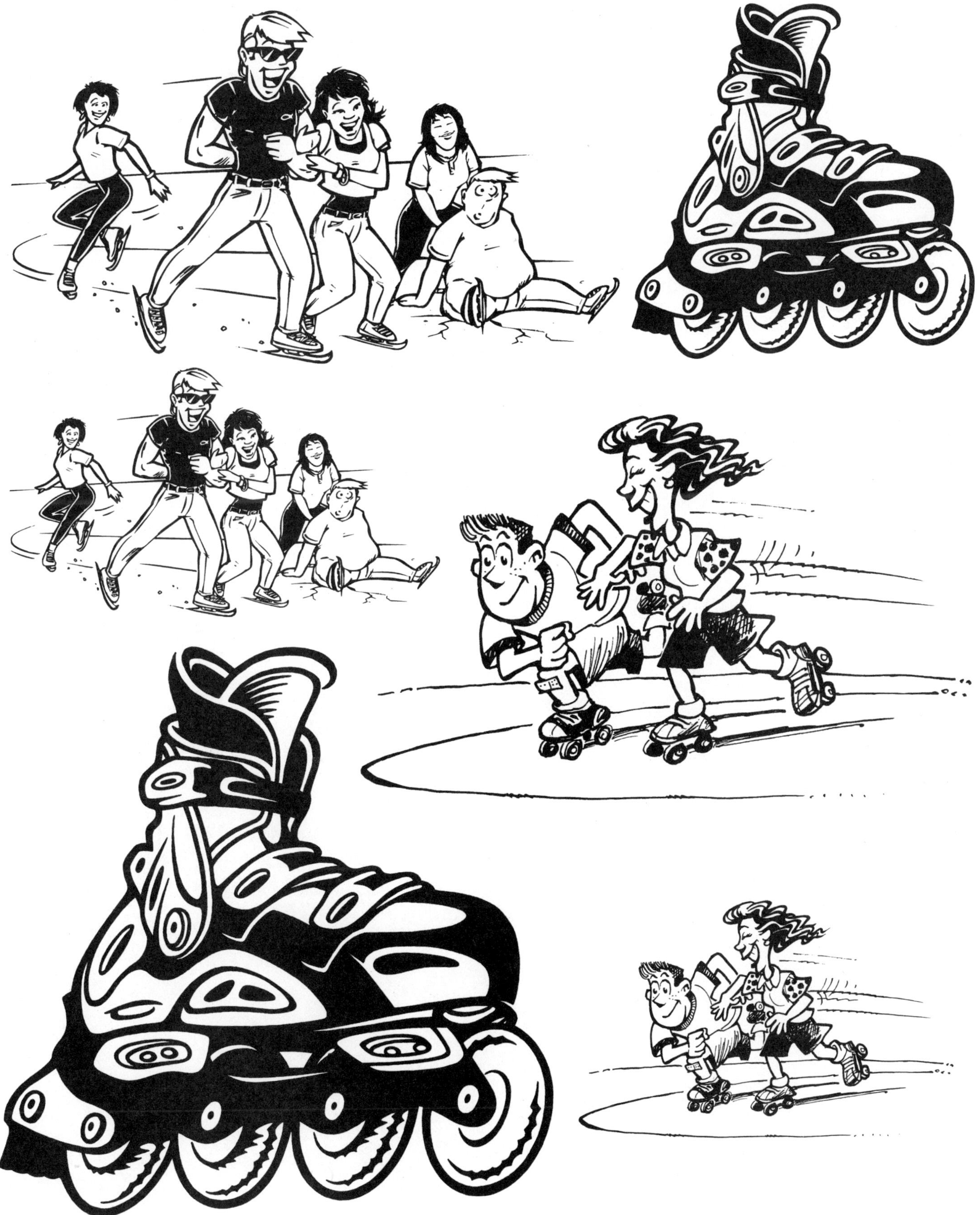

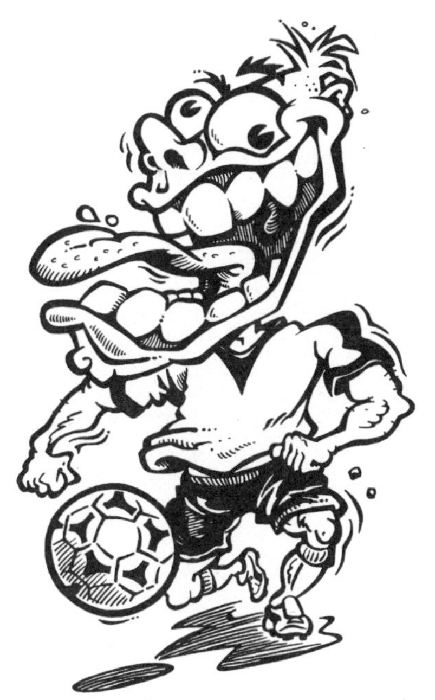

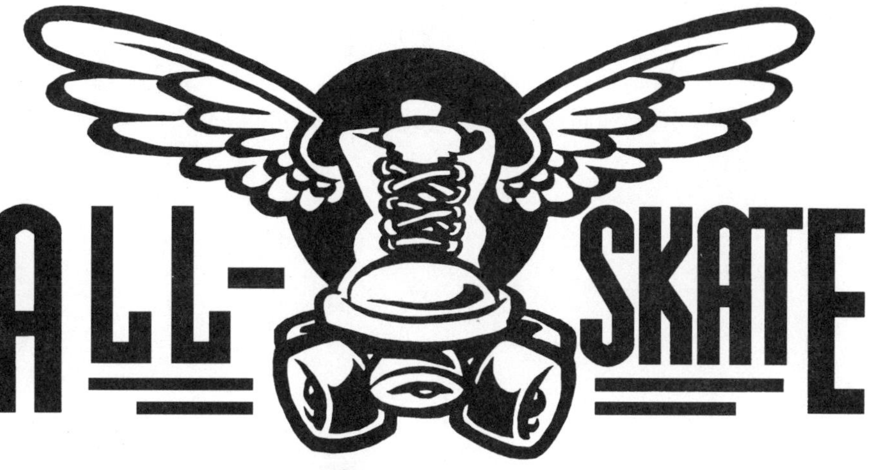
ALL-SKATE

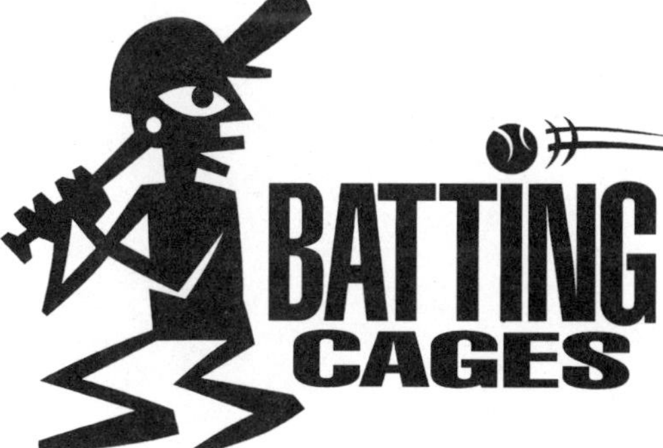
BATTING
CAGES

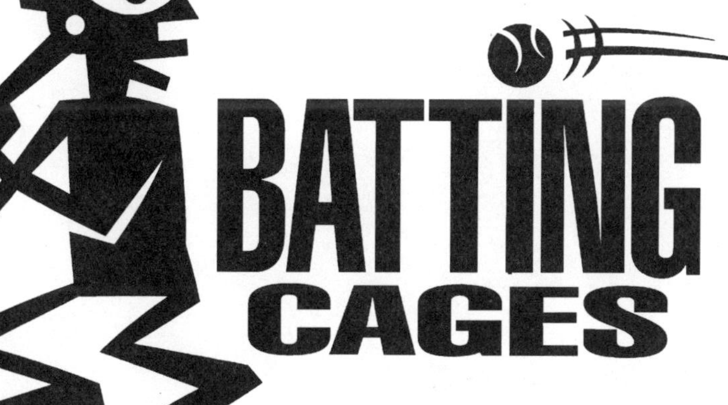
BATTING
CAGES

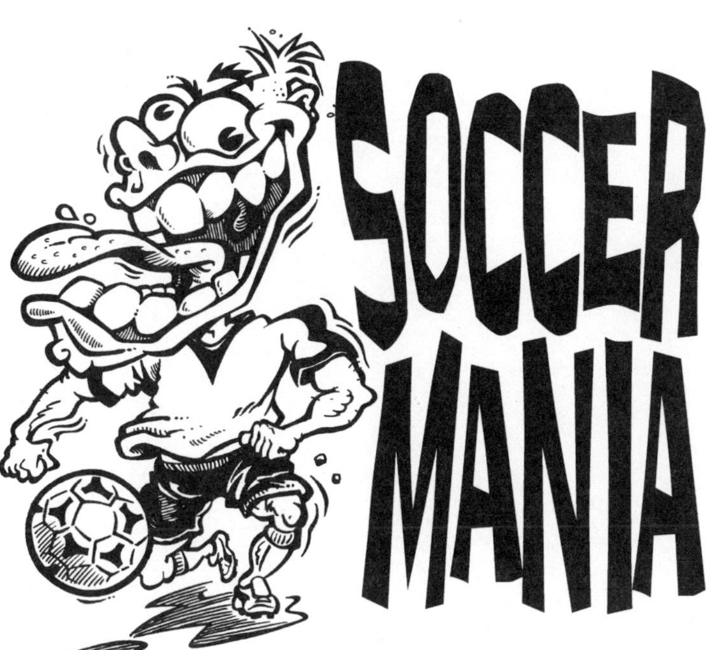
SOCCER
MANIA

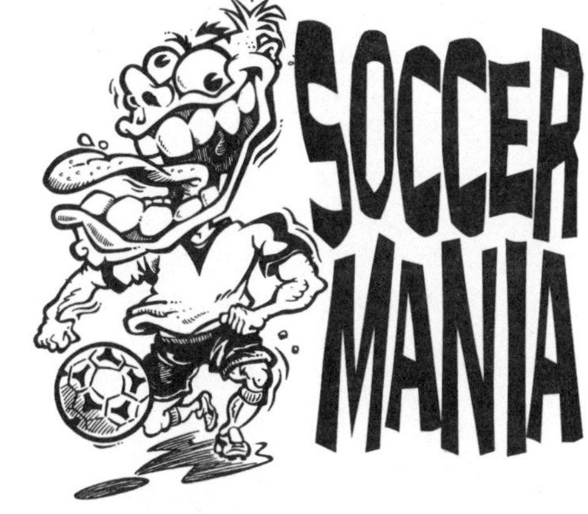
SOCCER
MANIA

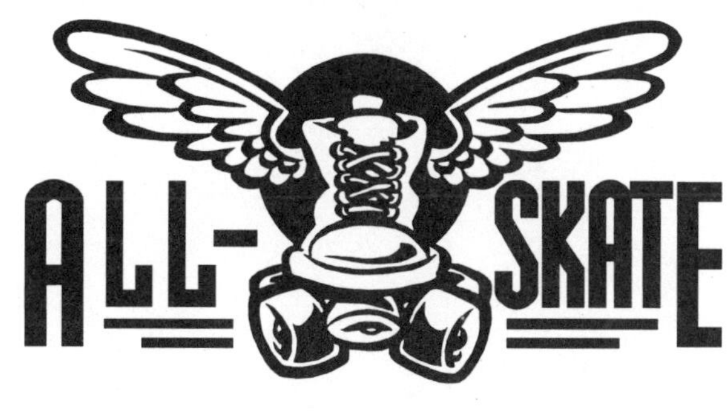
ALL-SKATE

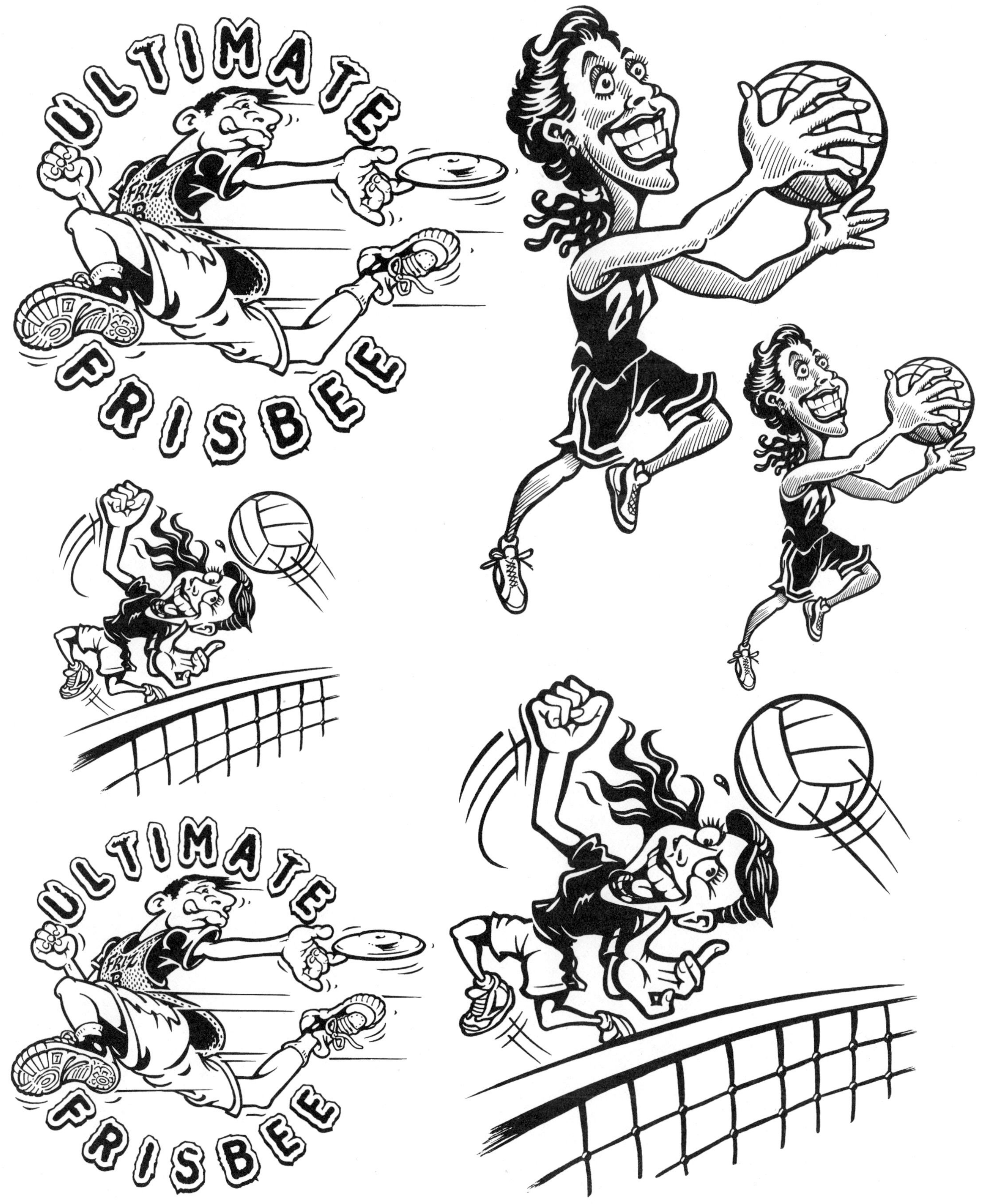
ULTIMATE
FRISBEE
ULTIMATE
FRISBEE

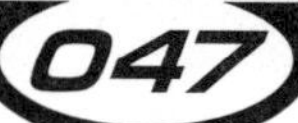

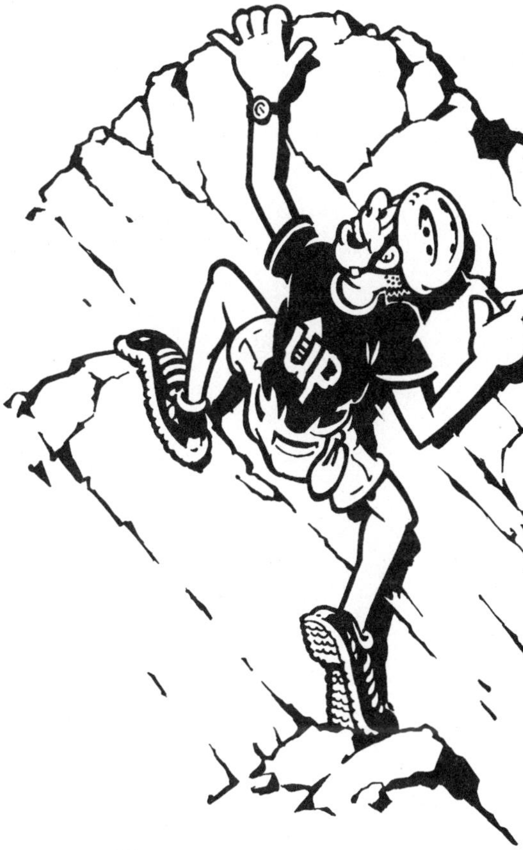

Summer Camp

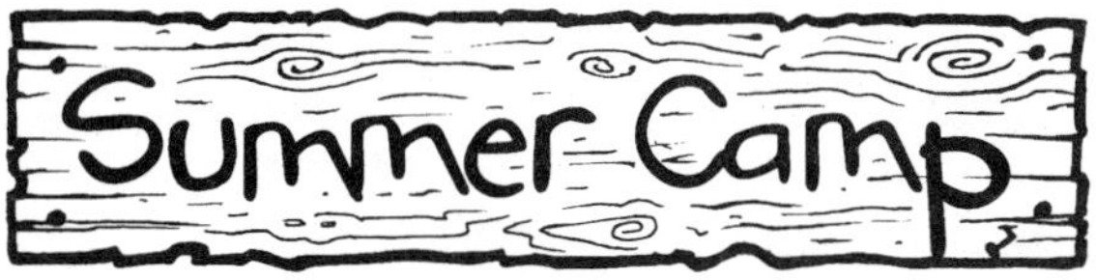

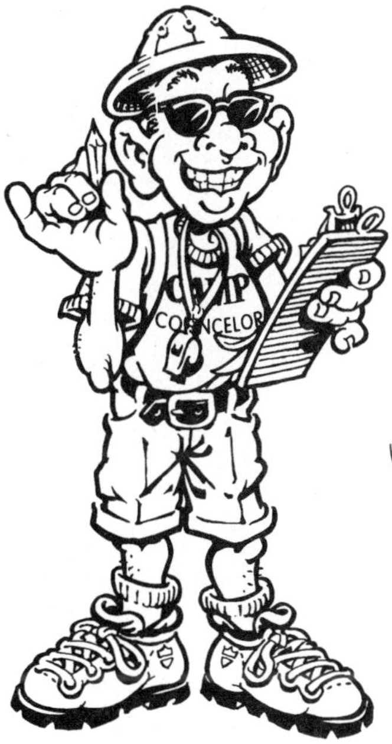

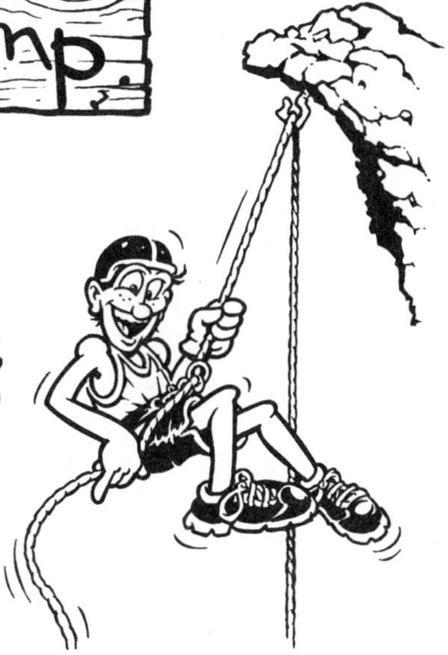

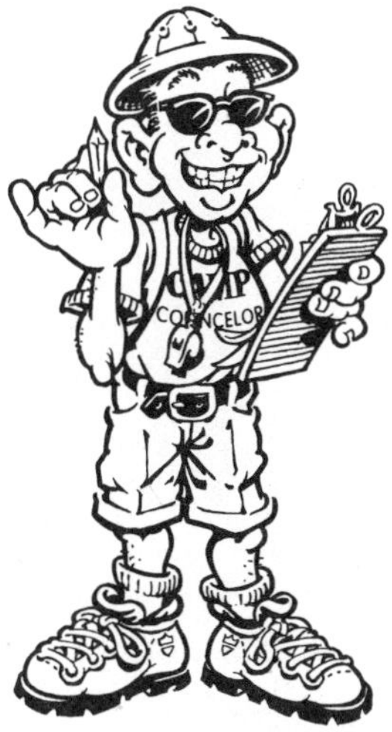

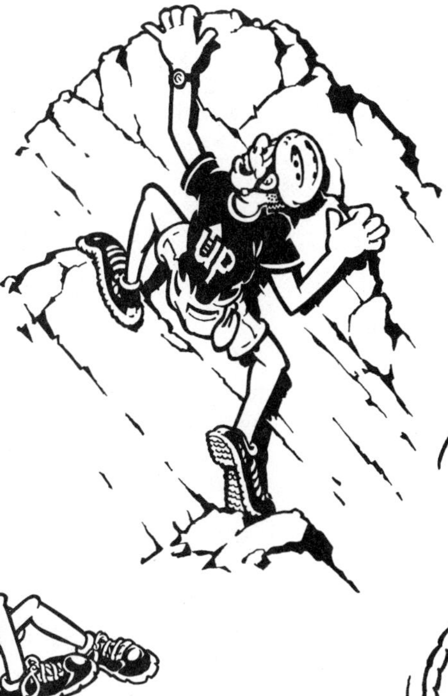

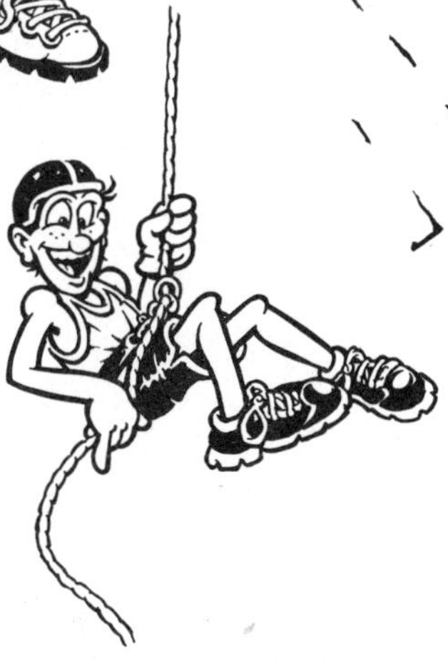

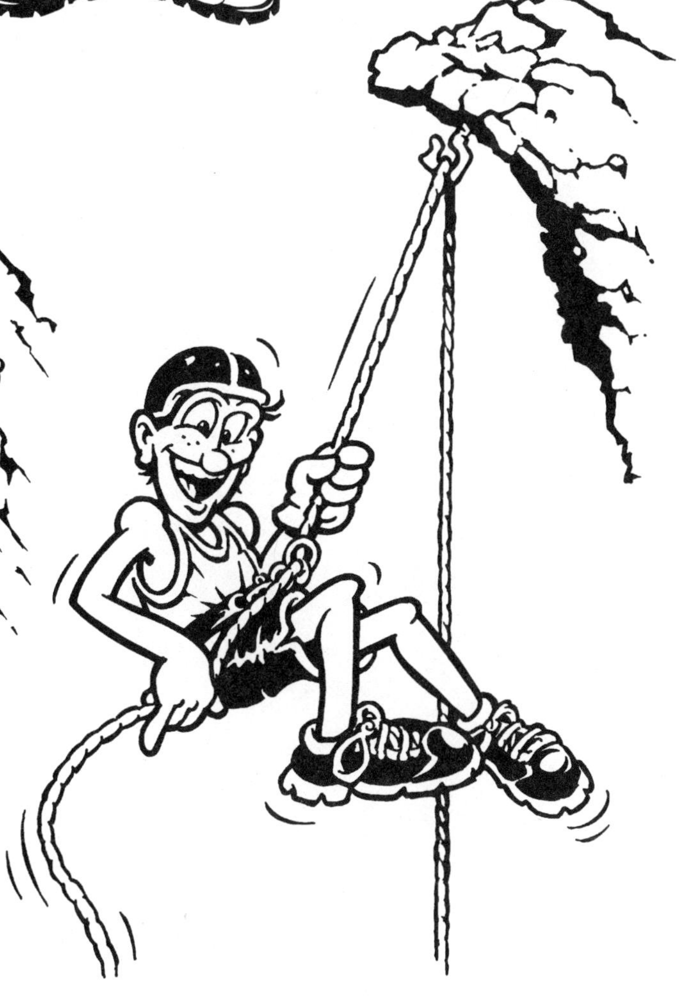

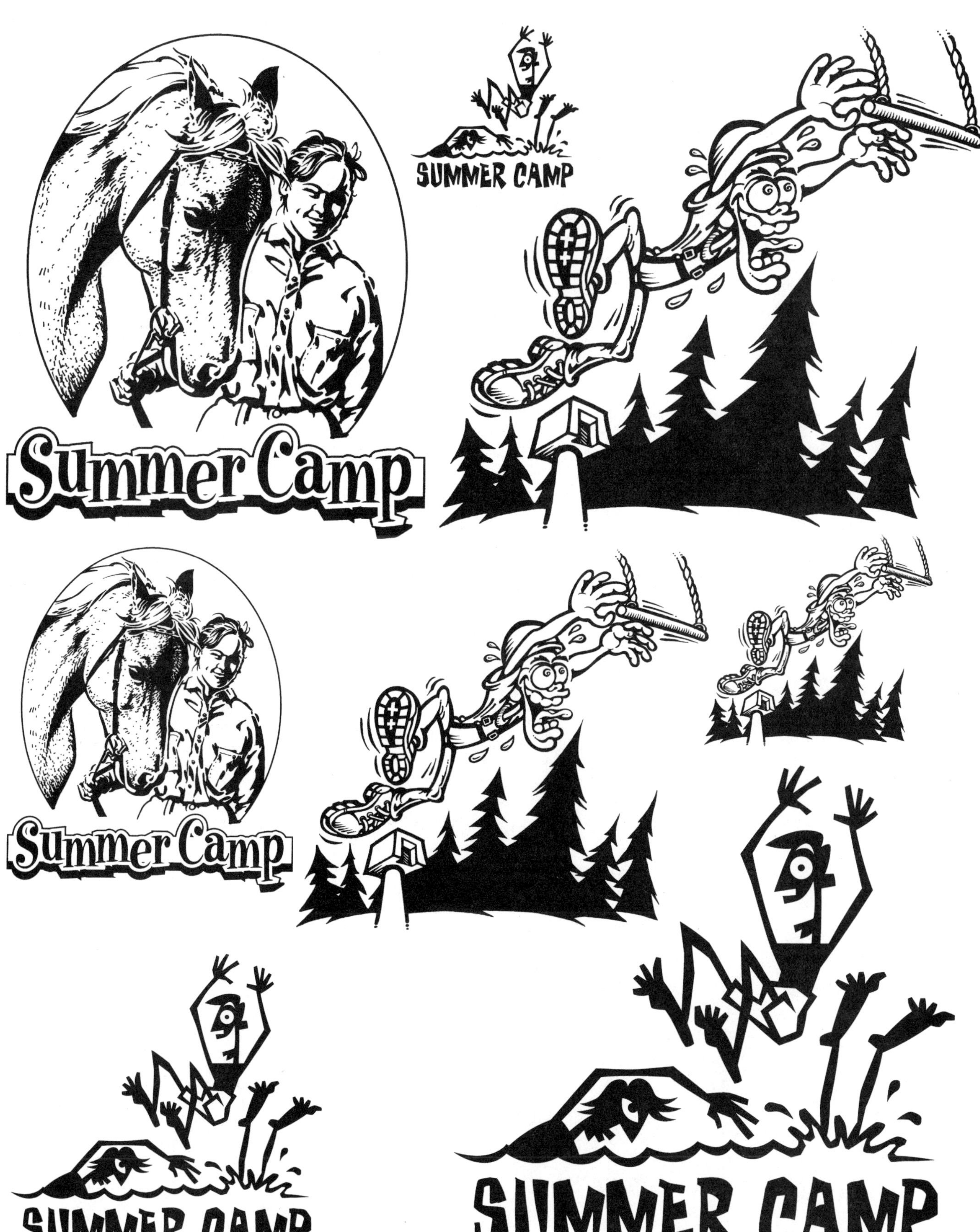
Summer Camp
SUMMER CAMP
Summer Camp
SUMMER CAMP
SUMMER CAMP

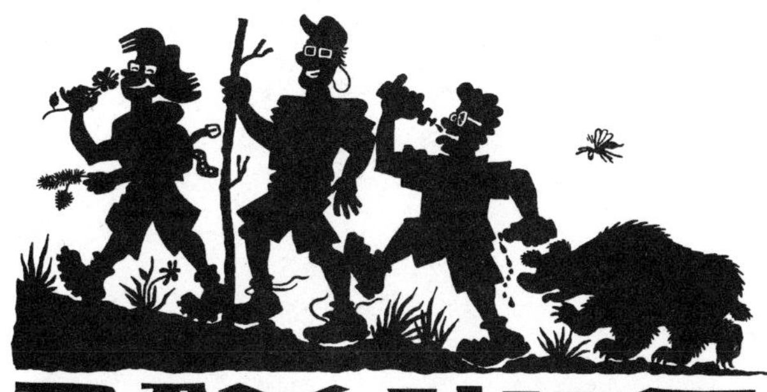

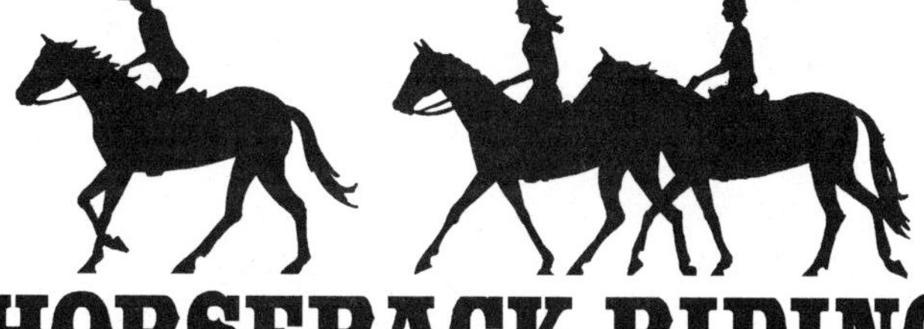

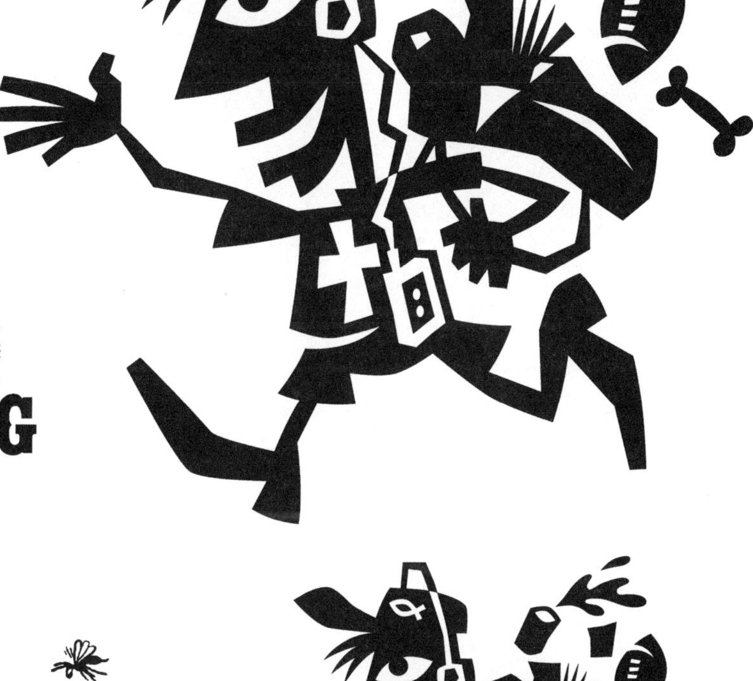

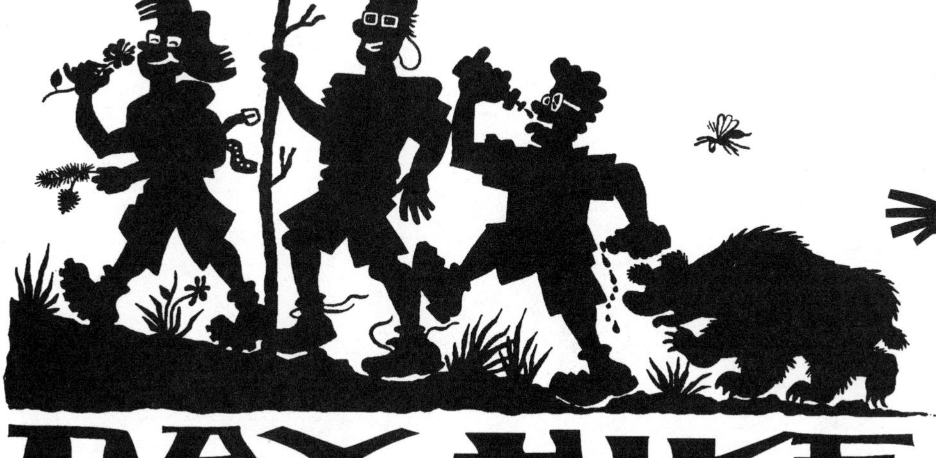

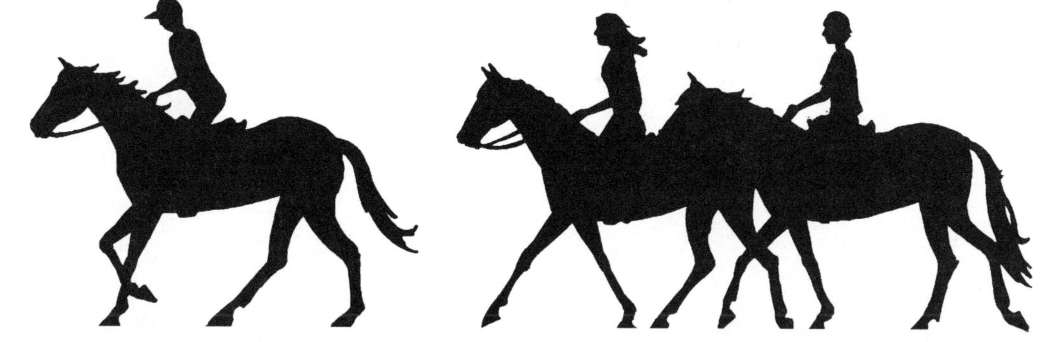

HORSEBACK RIDING

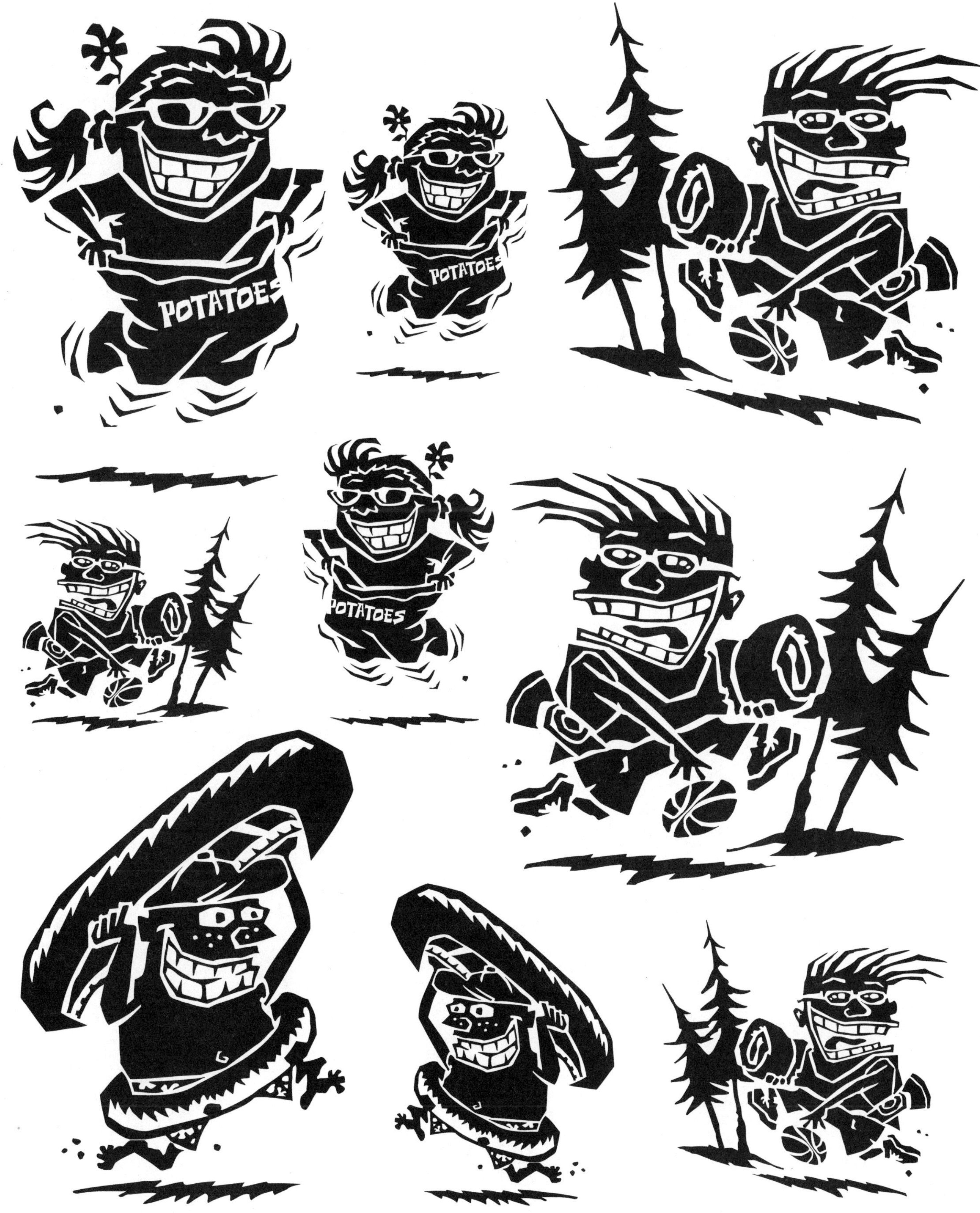
POTATOES
POTATOES
POTATOES

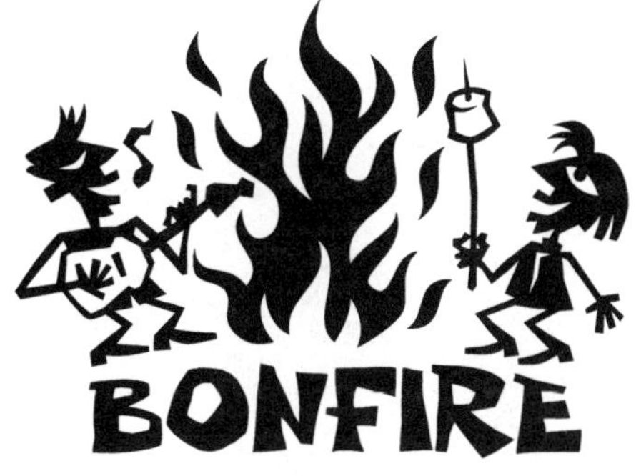
BONFIRE

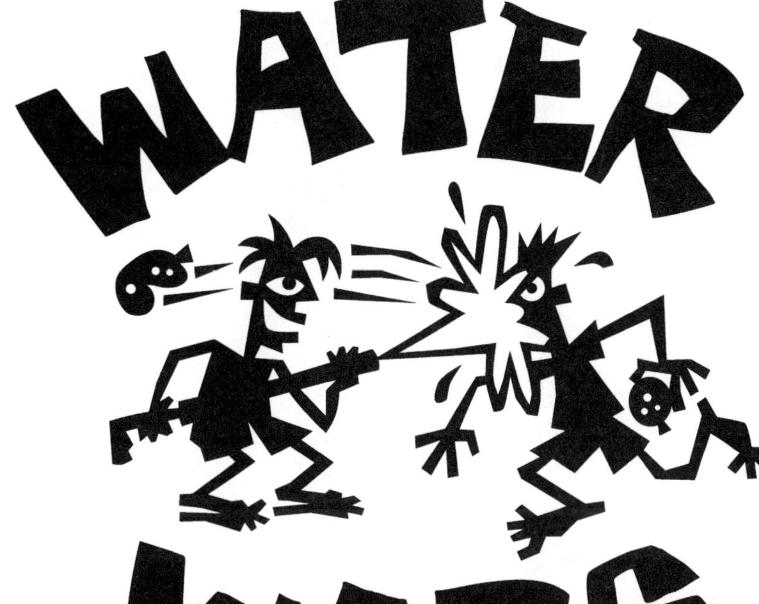
WATER
WARS

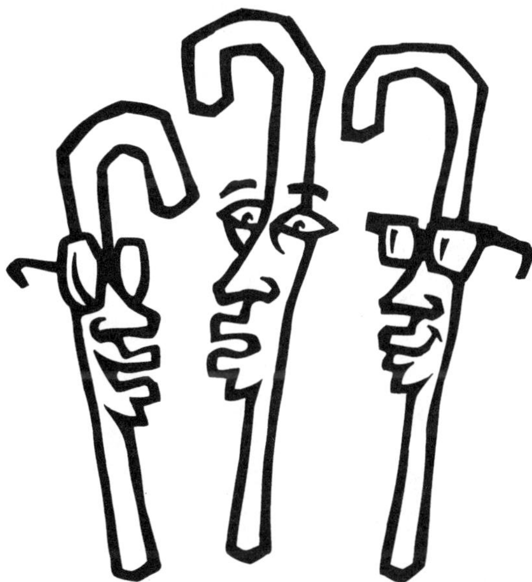
STAFF
RETREAT

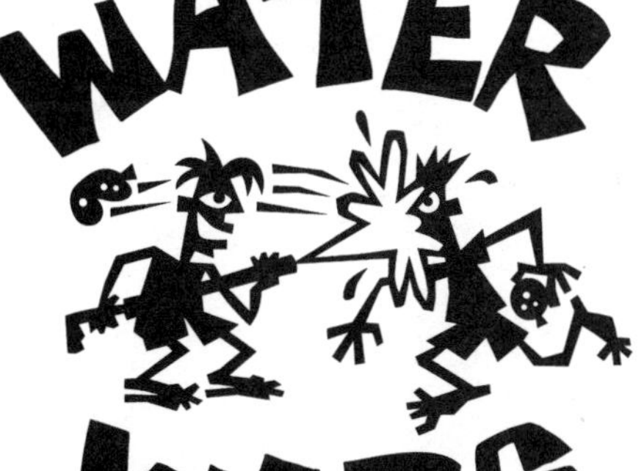
WATER
WARS

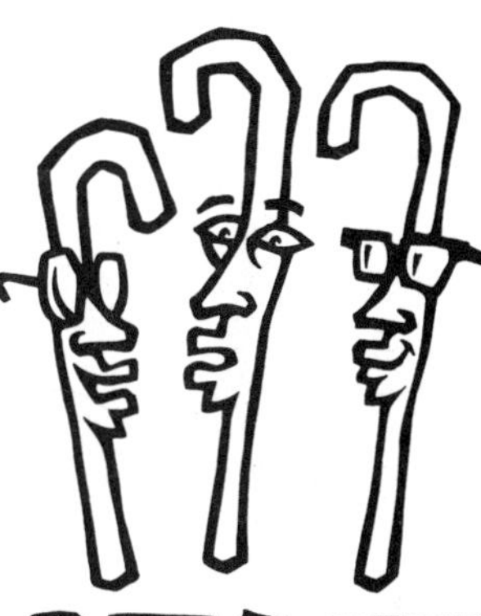
STAFF
RETREAT

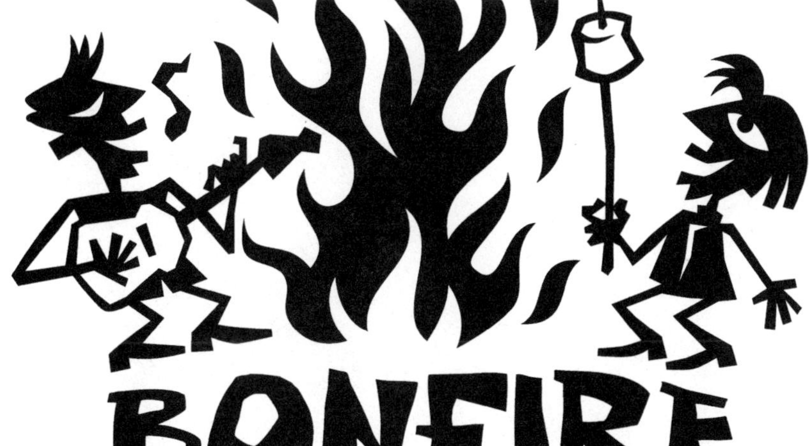
BONFIRE

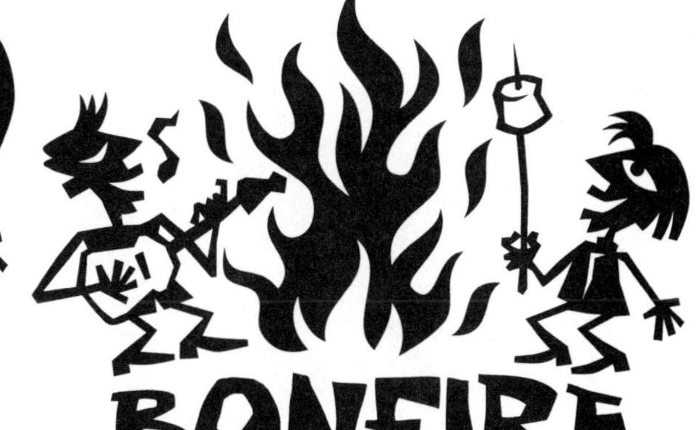
BONFIRE

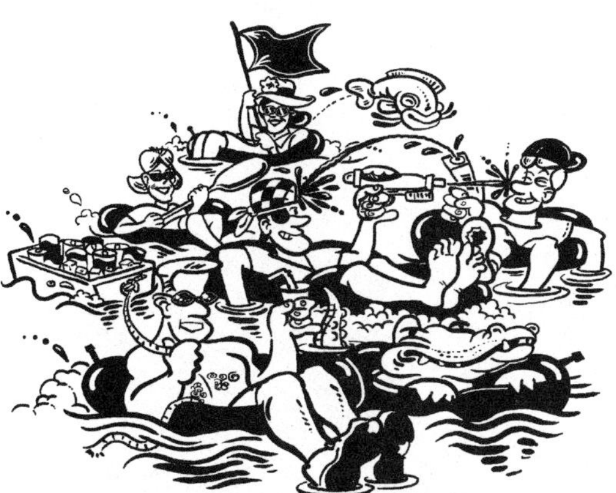

FLOAT TRIP

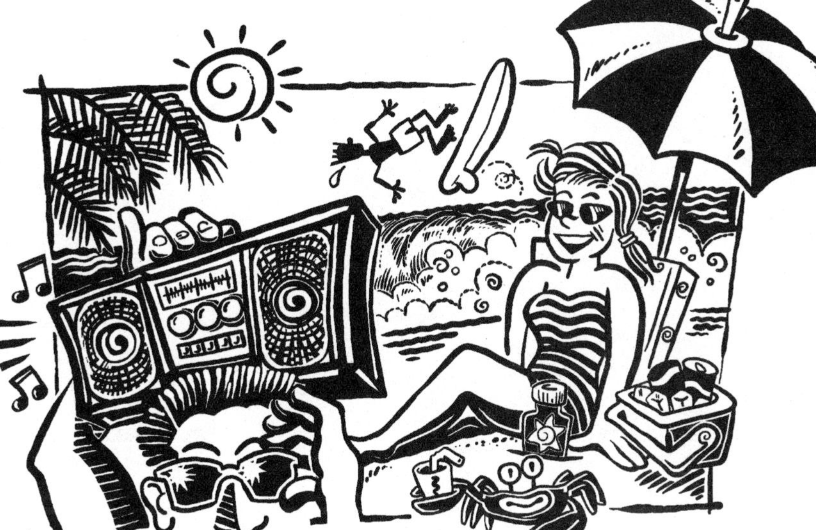

Beach Break

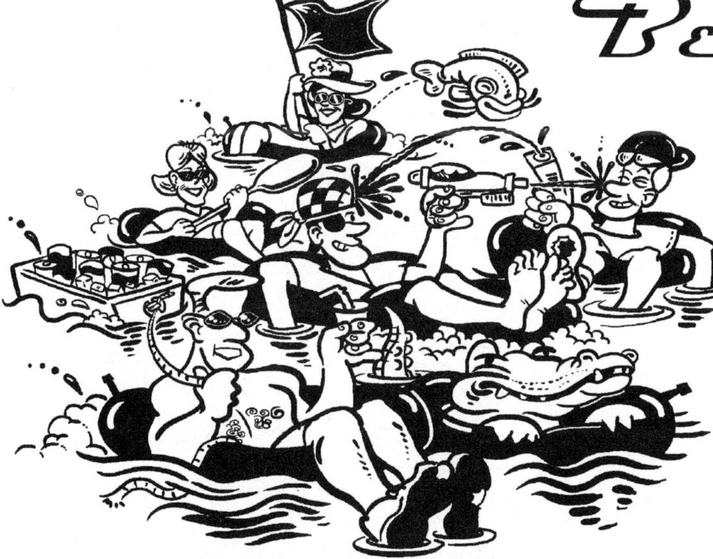

FLOAT TRIP

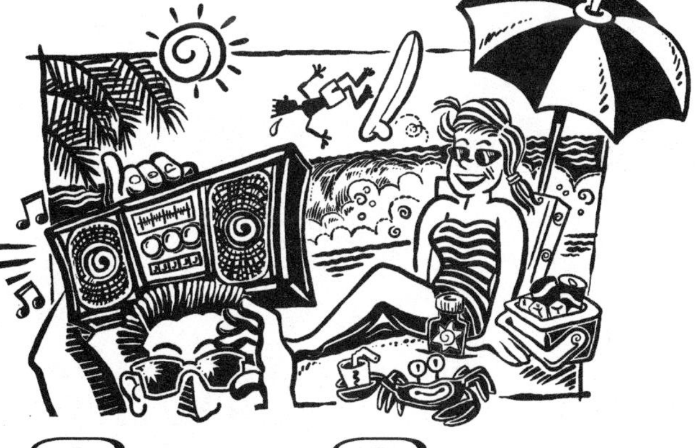

Beach Break

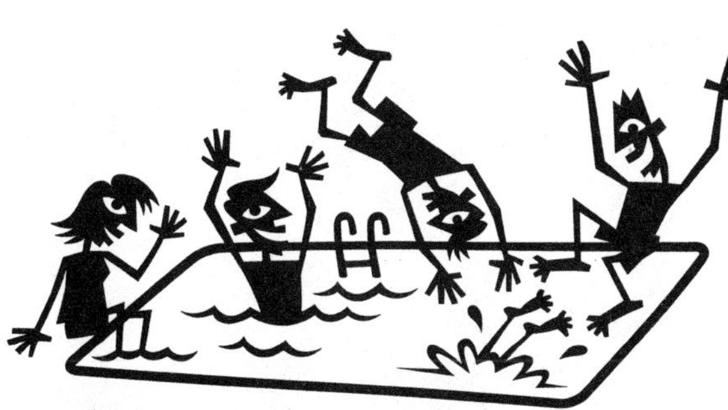

POOL PARTY

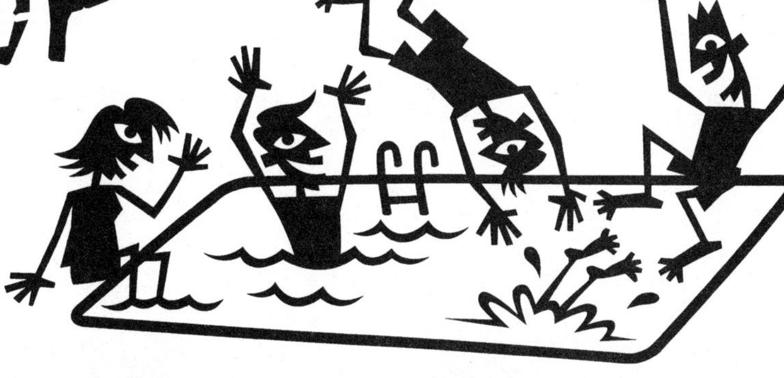

POOL PARTY

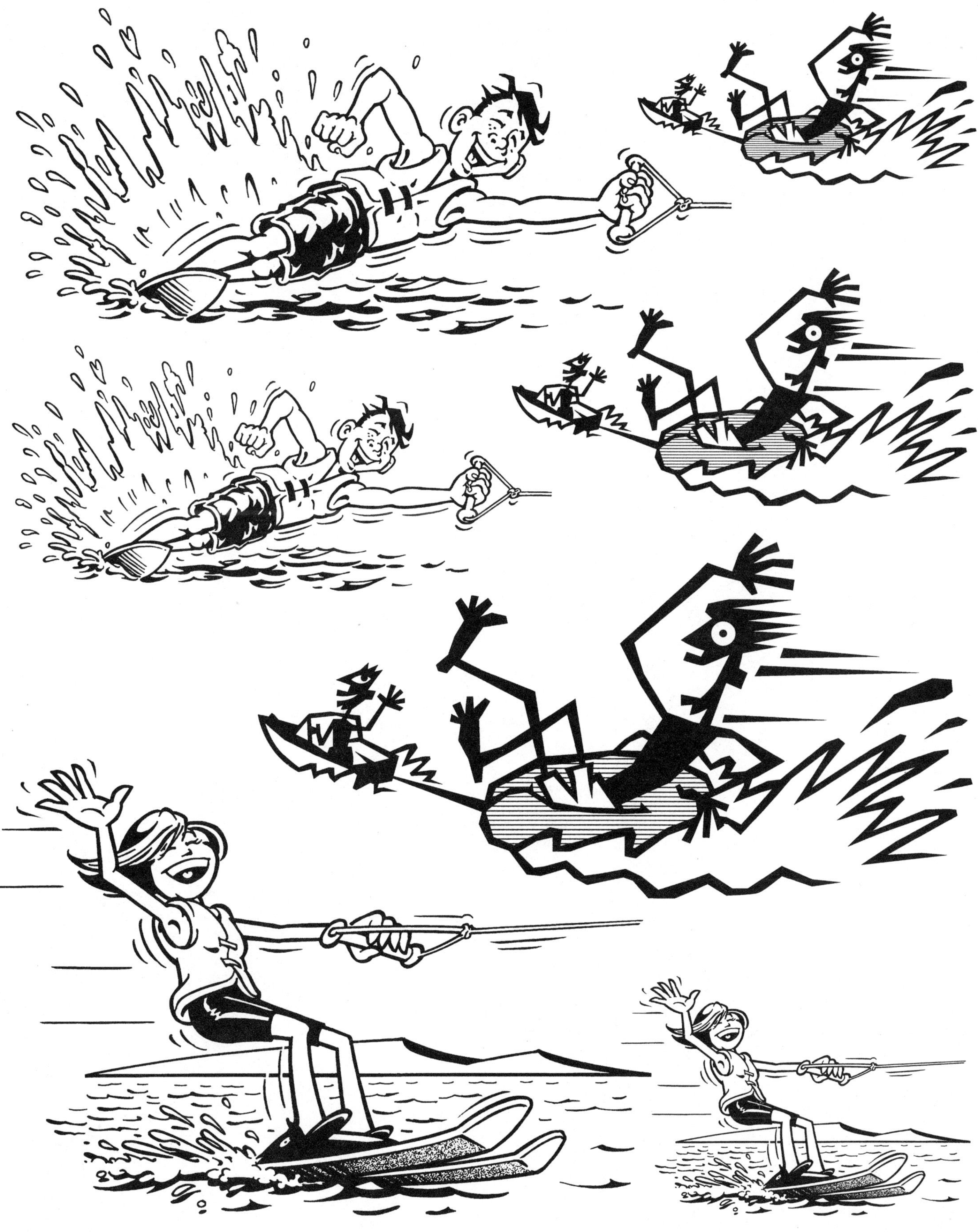

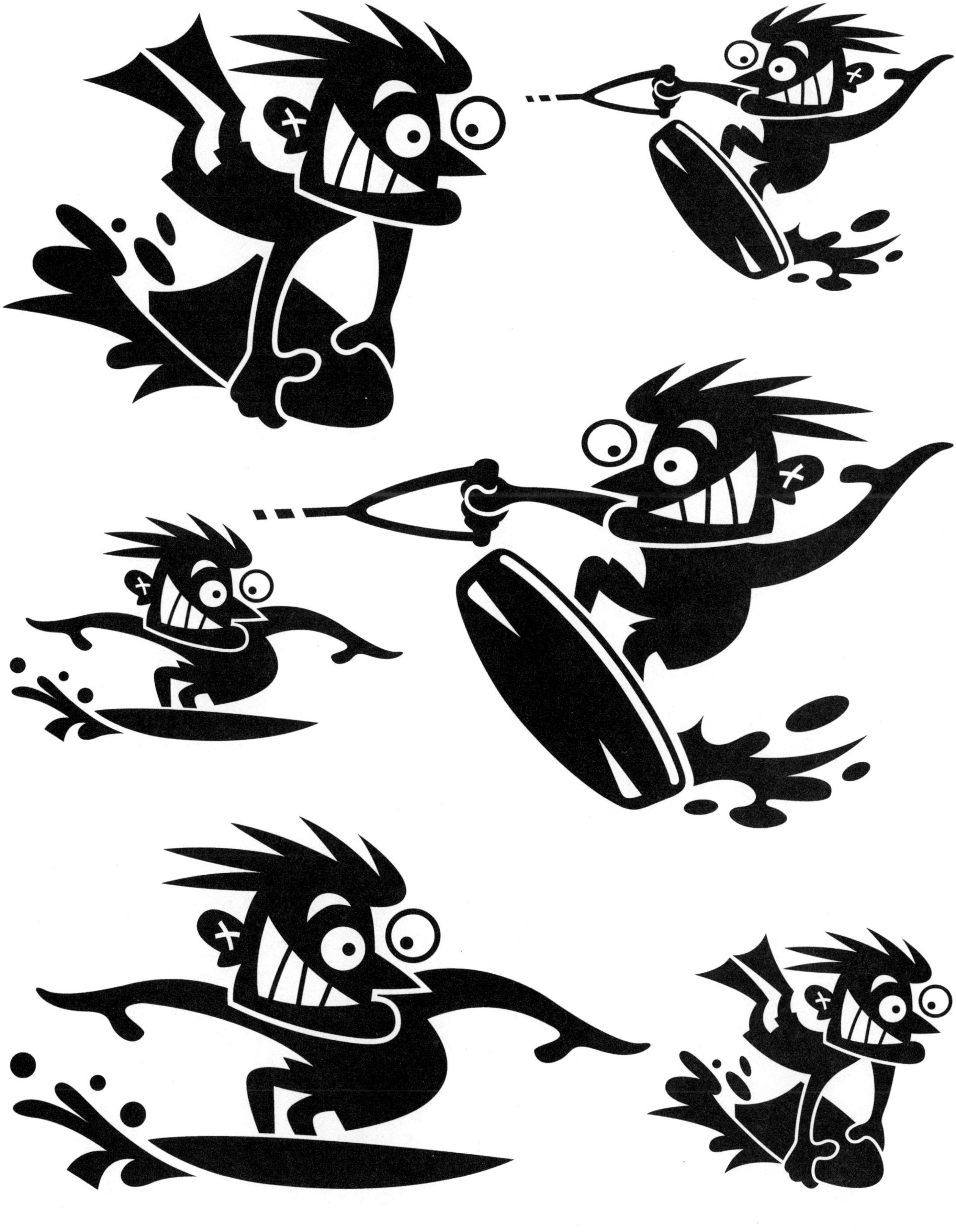

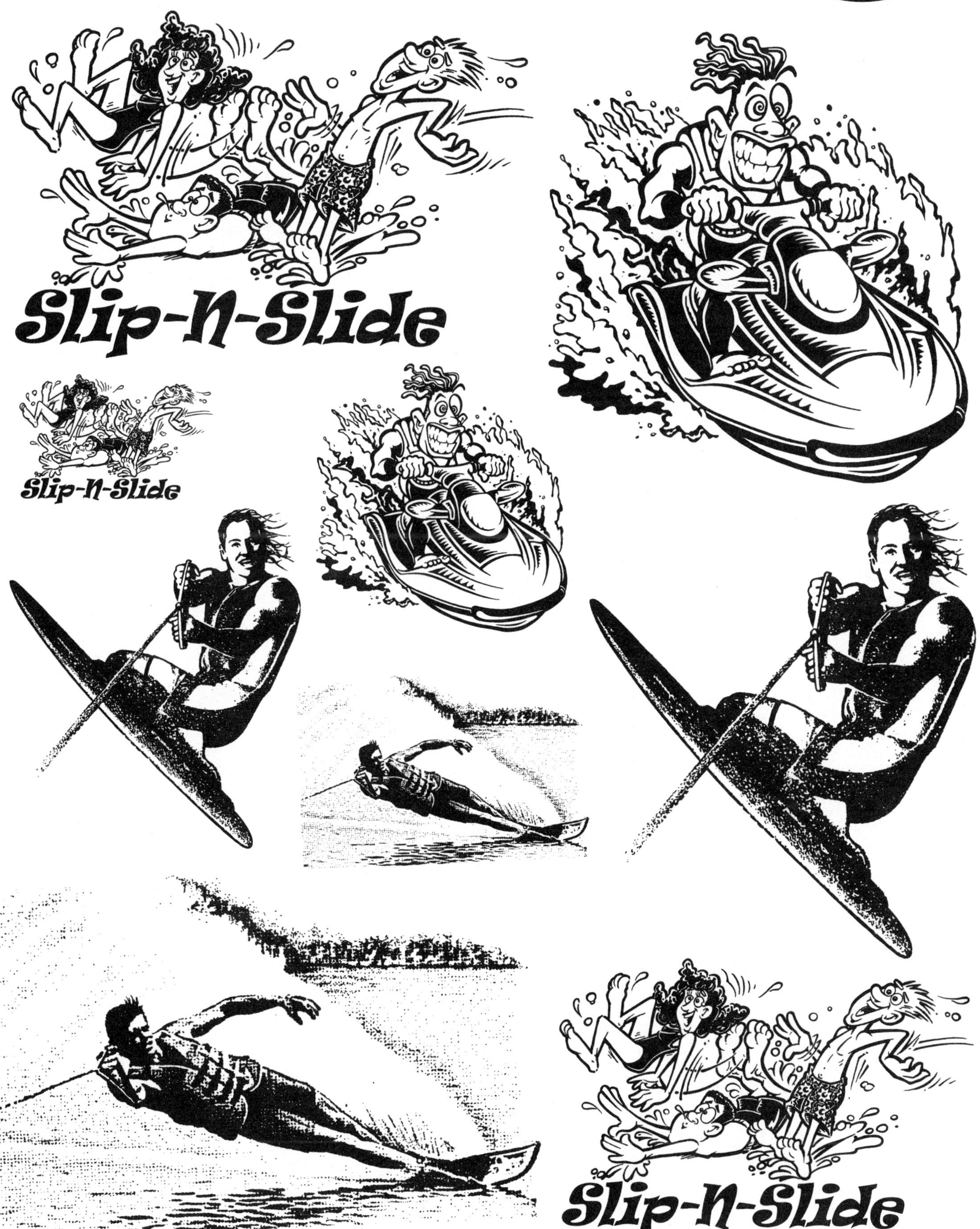
Slip-N-Slide
Slip-N-Slide
Slip-N-Slide

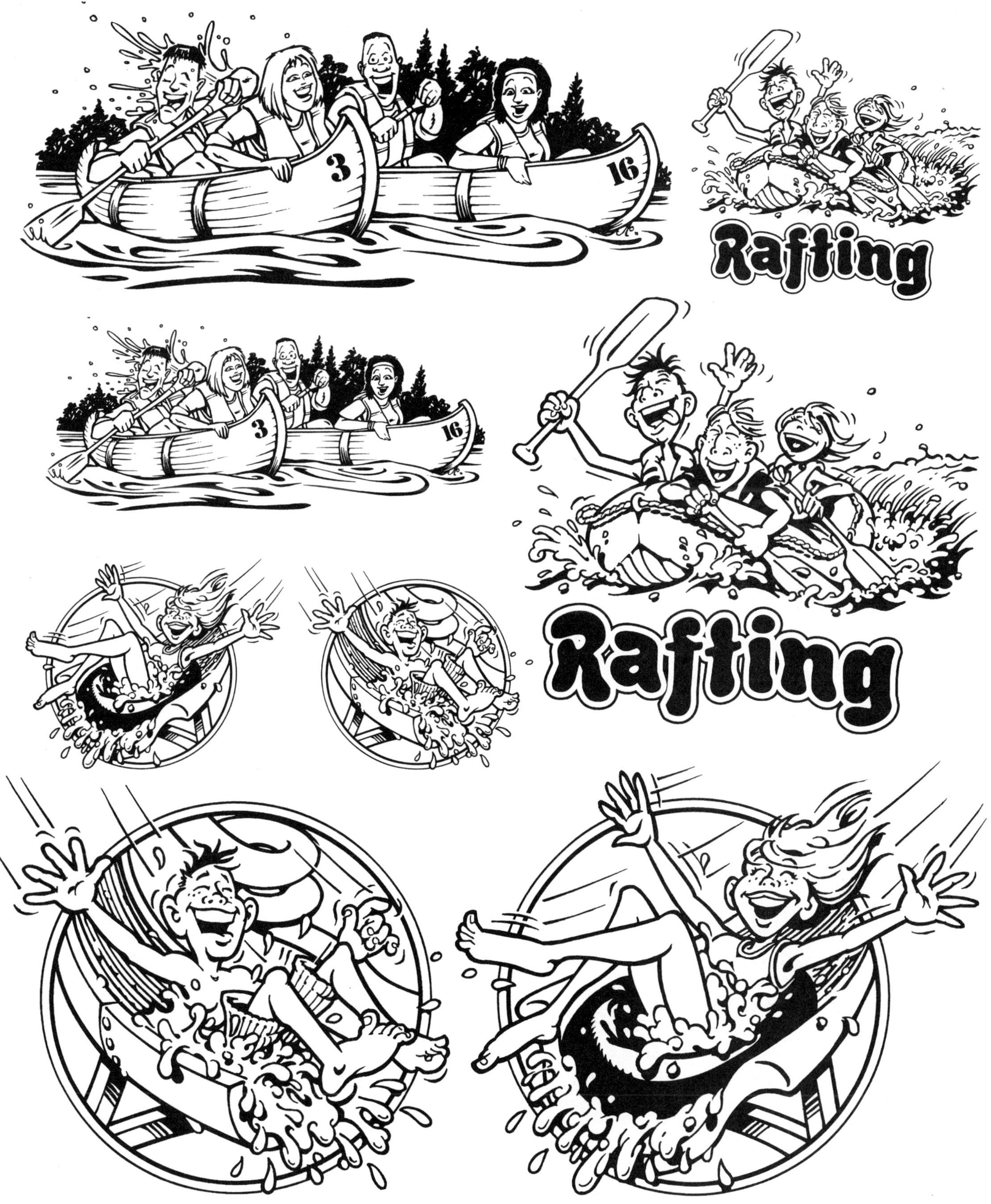
3
16
Rafting
3
16
Rafting

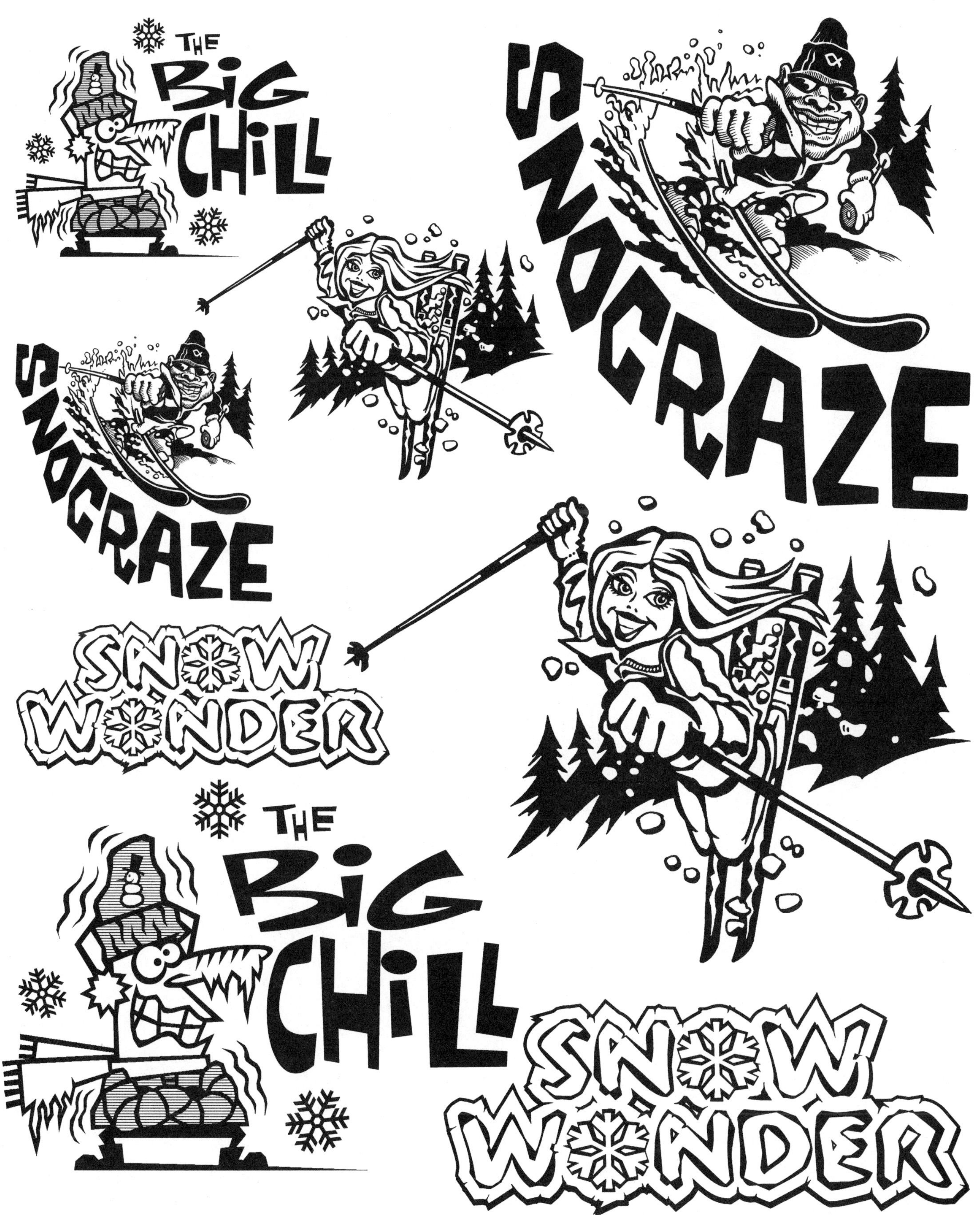
THE
BIG
CHILL
SNOGRAZE
SNOGRAZE
SNOW
WONDER
THE
BIG
CHILL
SNOW
WONDER

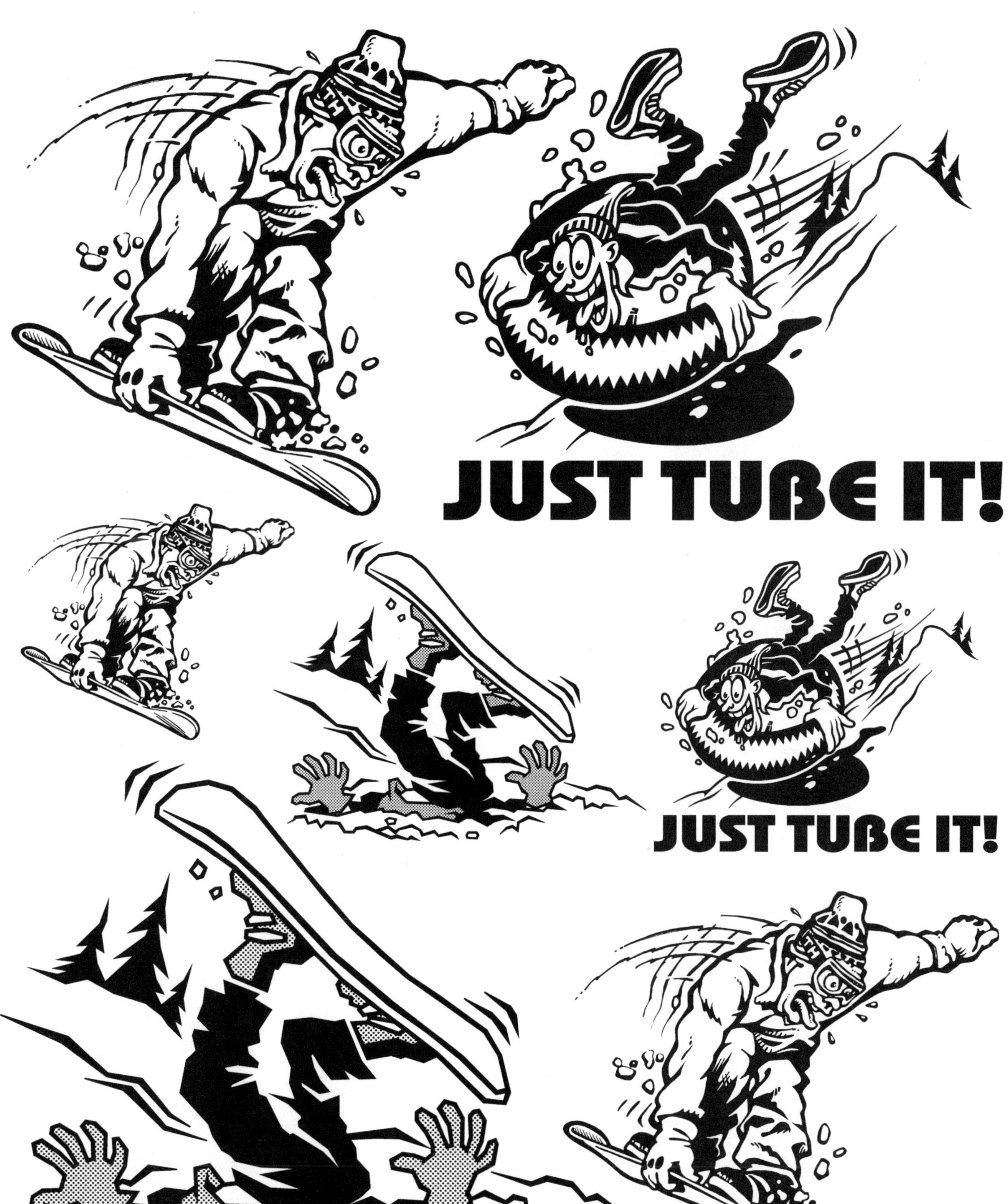
JUST TUBE IT!
JUST TUBE IT!

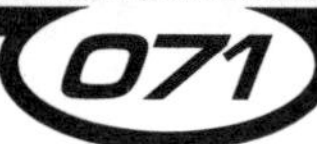

HOBO PARTY

mid winter
BEACH PARTY

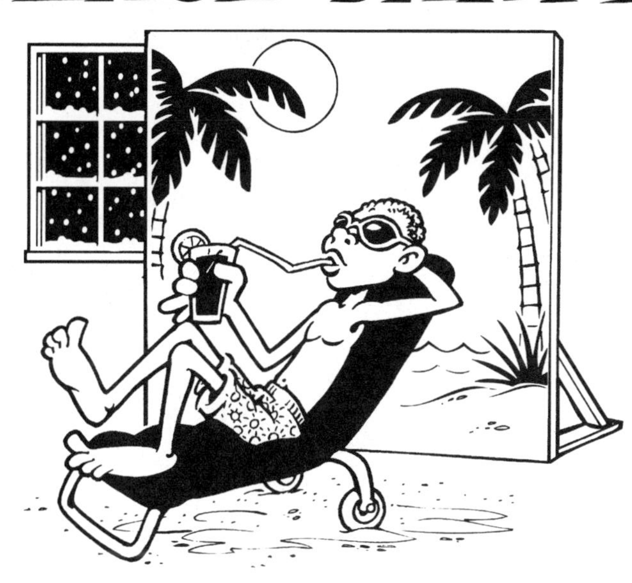

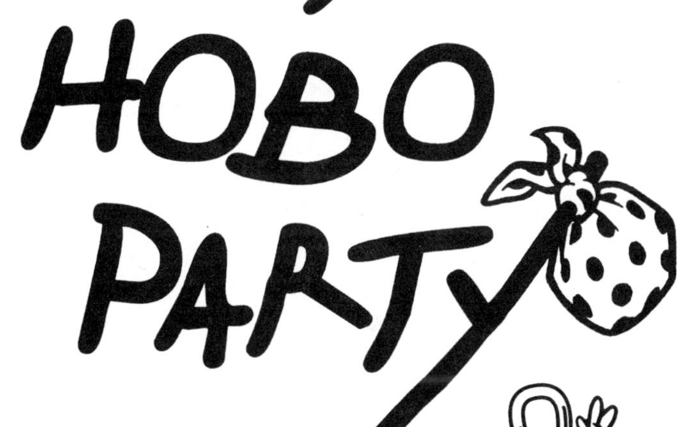

LOCK-IN

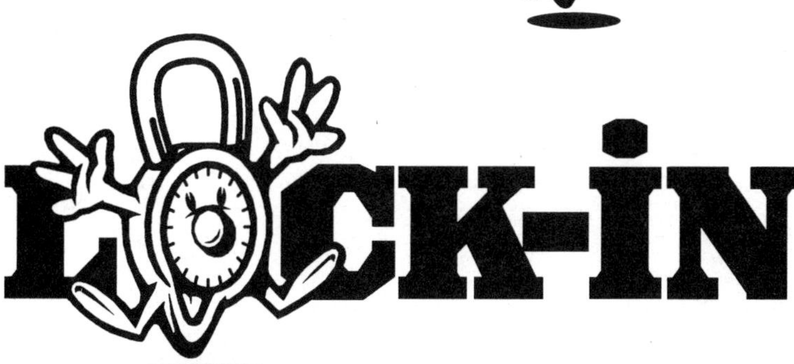

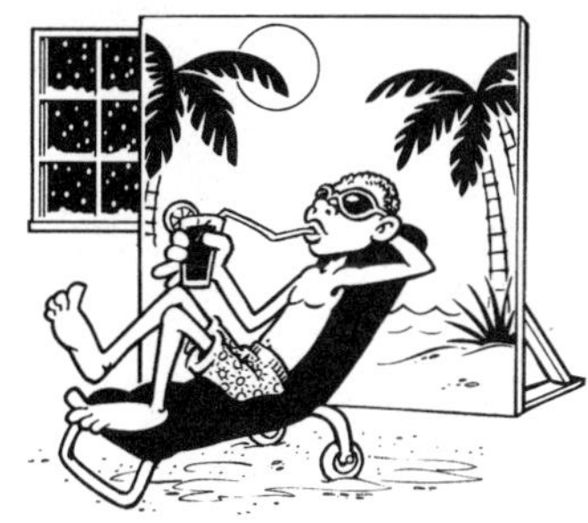

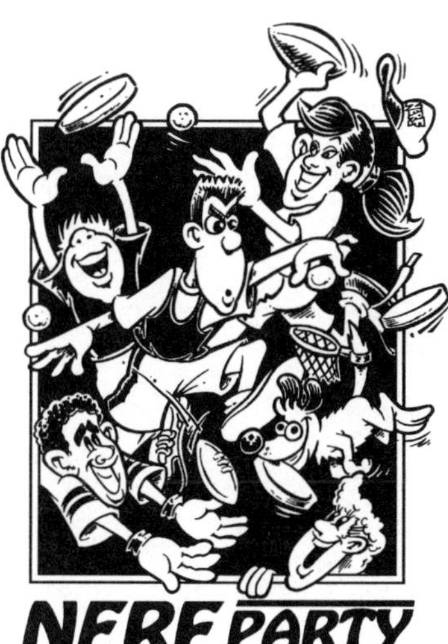

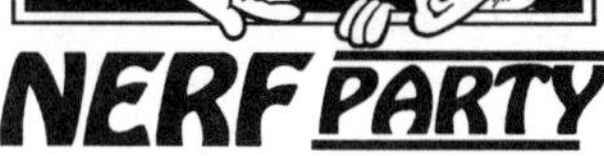

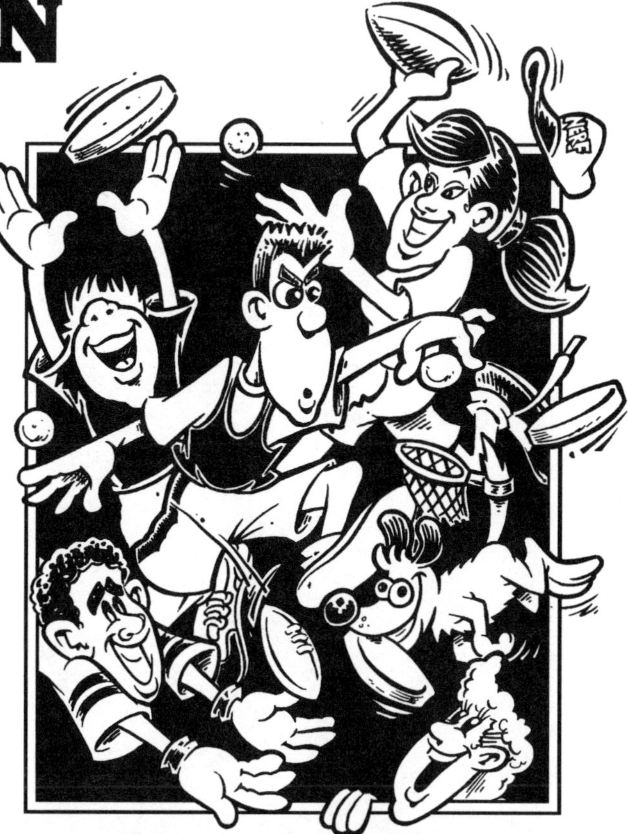

NERF PARTY

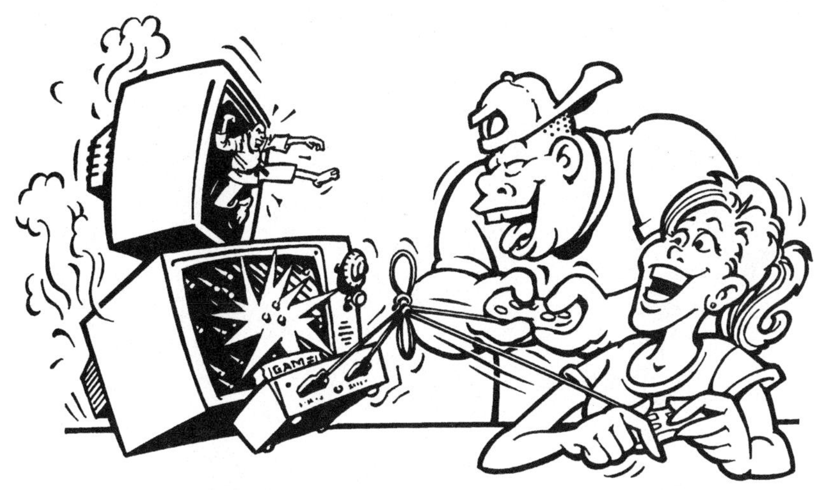
GAME
Nintendo
NIGHT

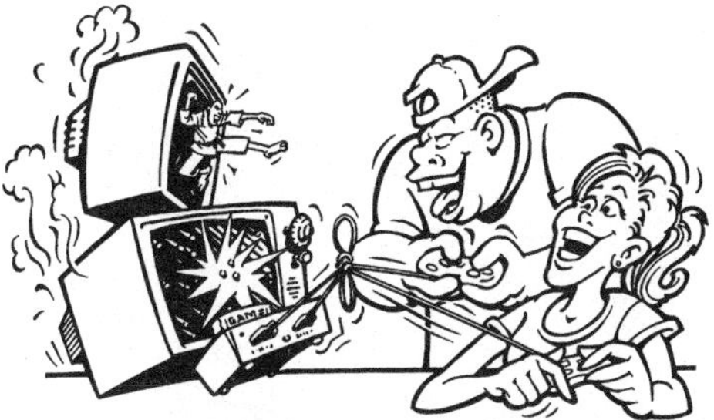
Nintendo
NIGHT

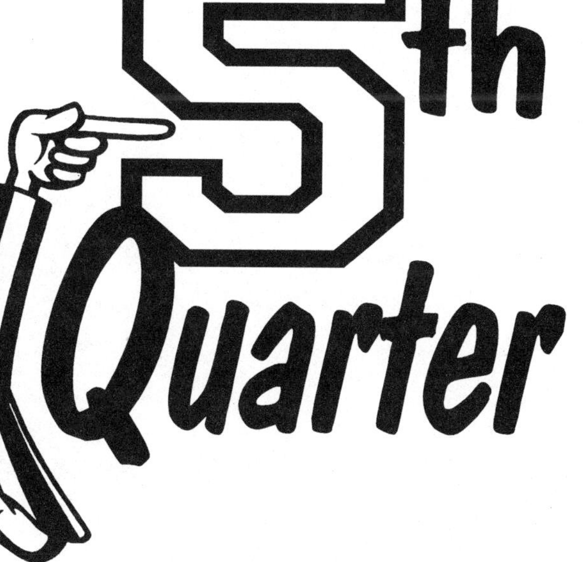
5th
Quarter

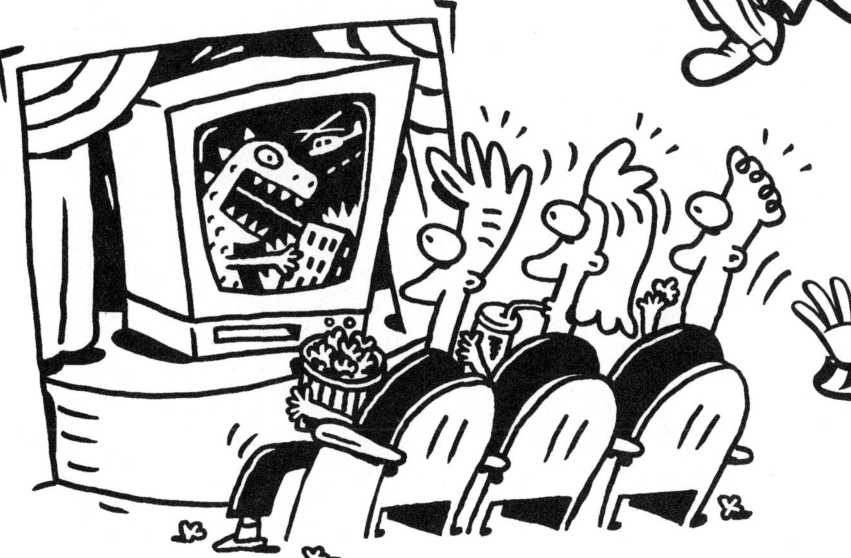

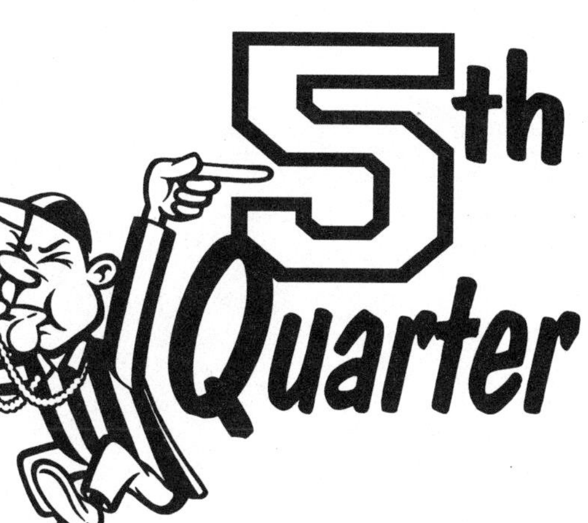
5th
Quarter

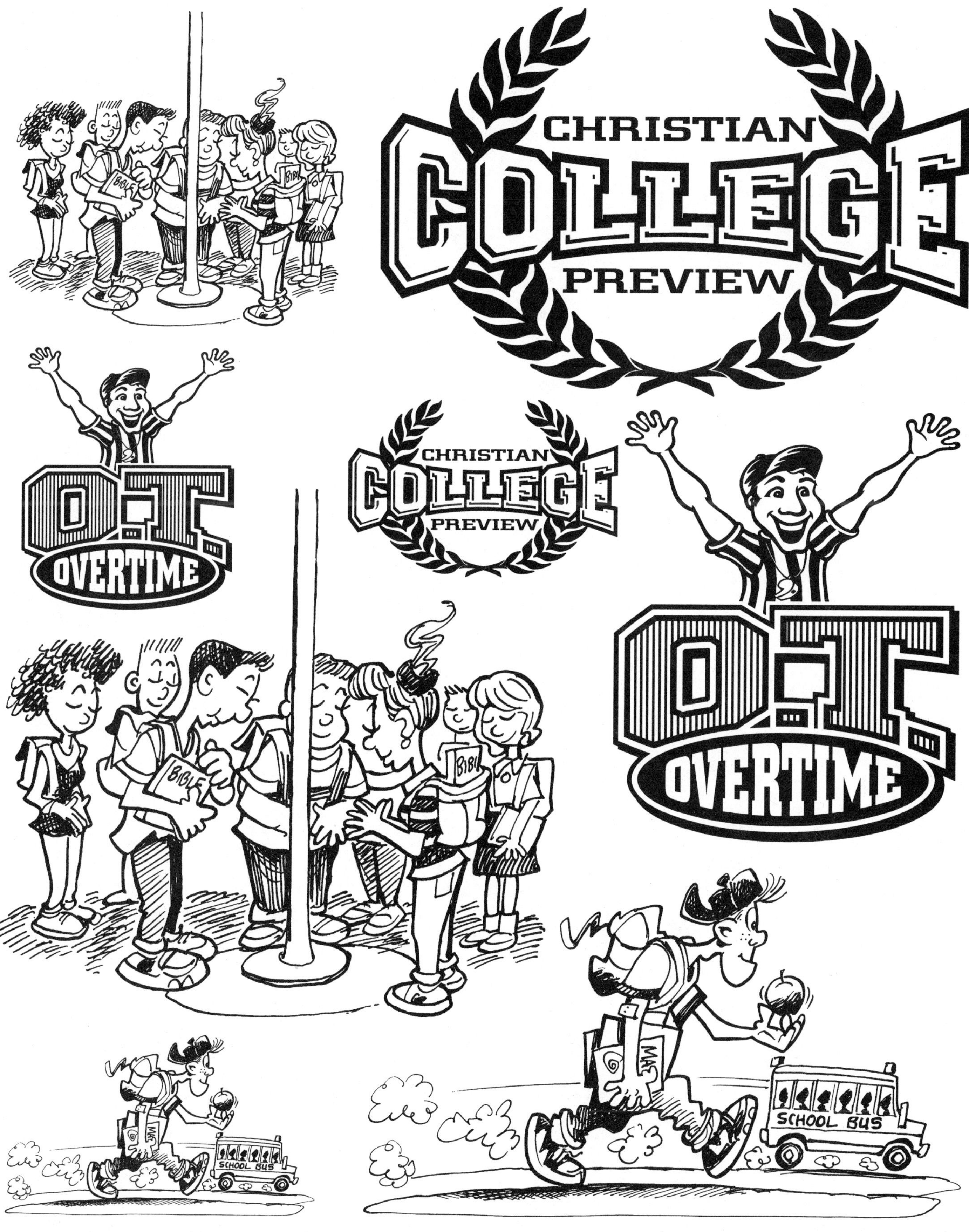
CHRISTIAN
COLLEGE
PREVIEW
BIBLE
BIBLE
O.T.
OVERTIME
CHRISTIAN
COLLEGE
PREVIEW
O.T.
OVERTIME
BIBLE
BIBLE
SCHOOL BUS
SCHOOL BUS

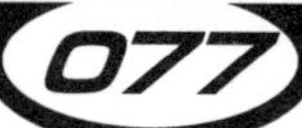

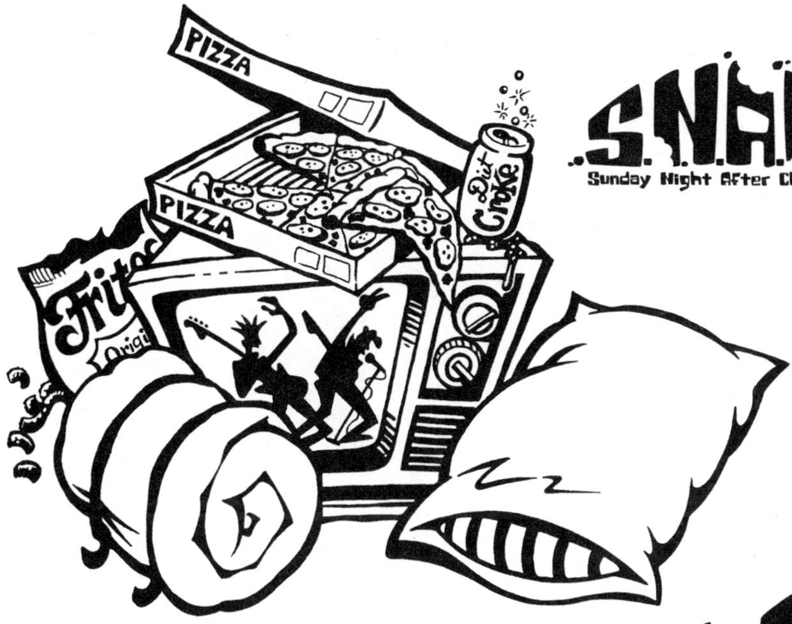

S.N.A.C.
Sunday Night After Church

? Dating Game

OVERNIGHTER

S.N.A.C.
Sunday Night After Church

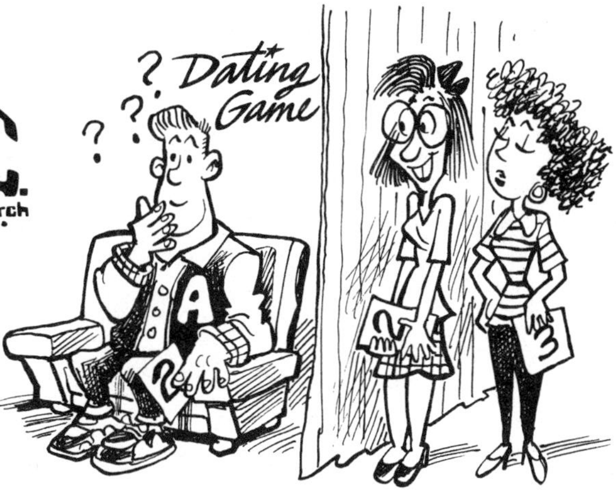

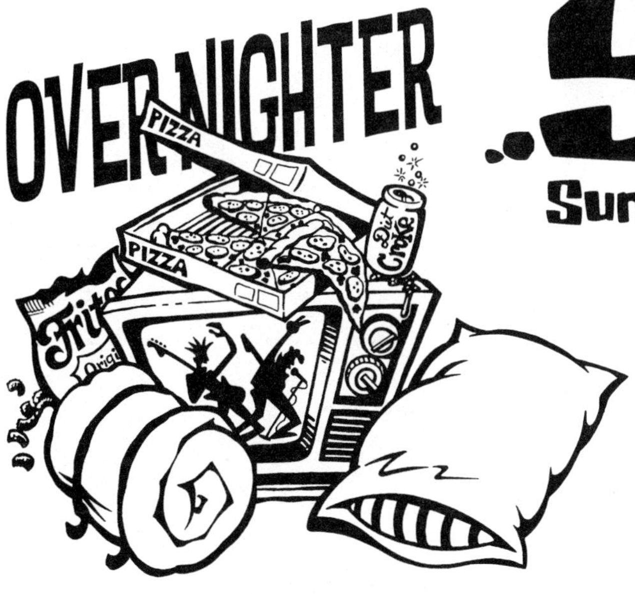

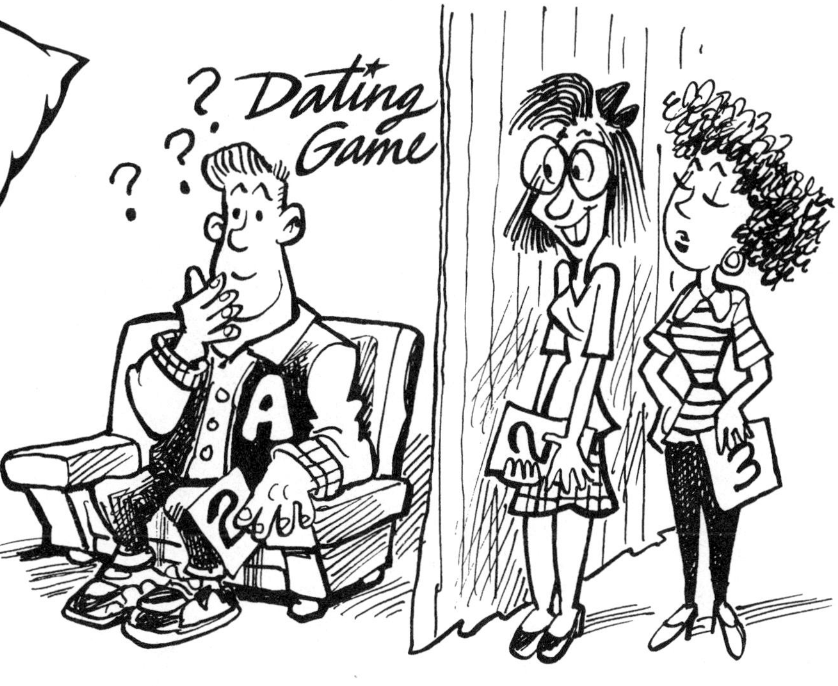

? Dating Game

S.N.A.C.
Sunday Night After Church

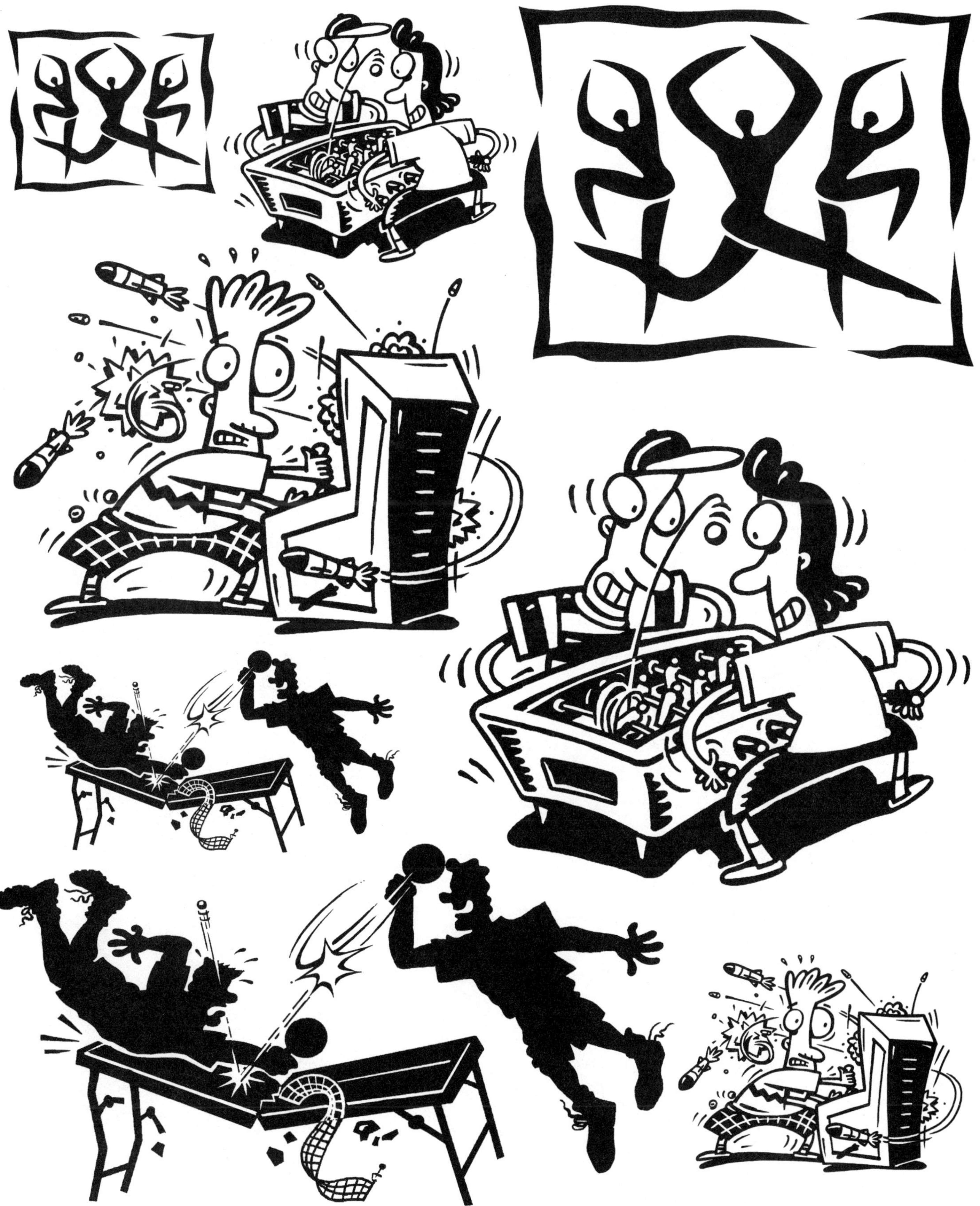

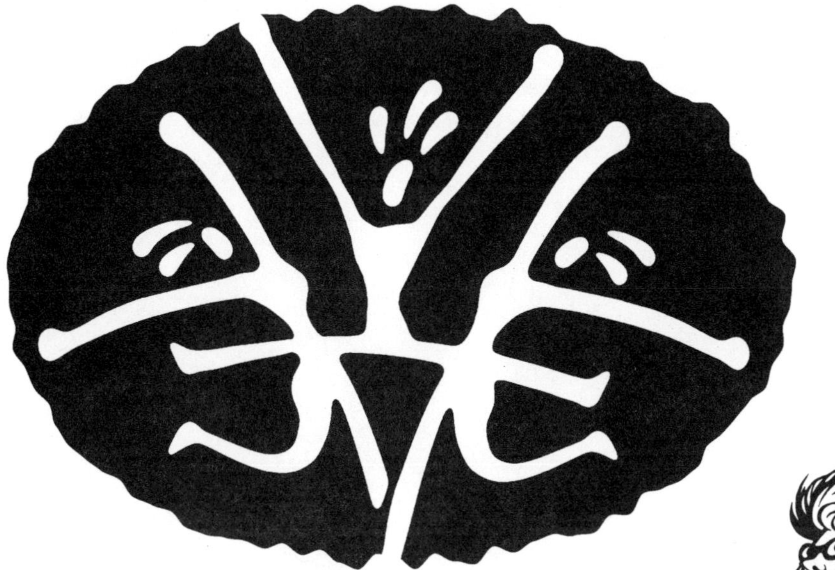

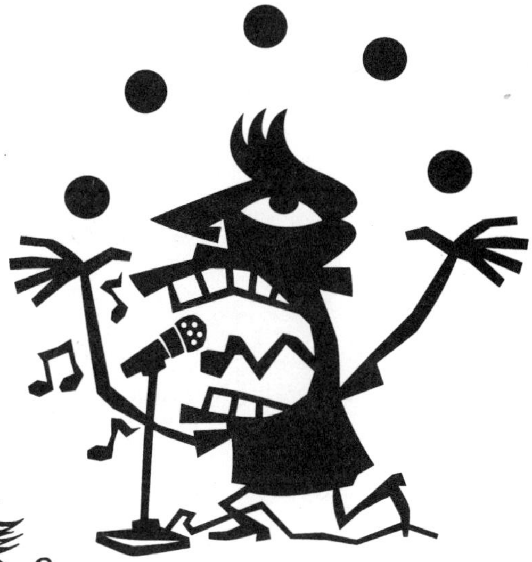

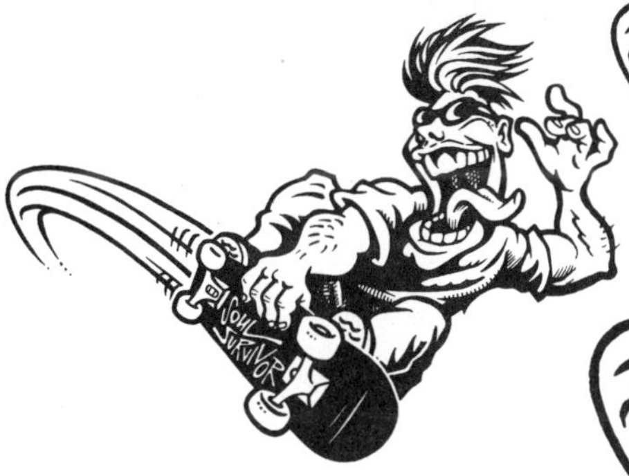

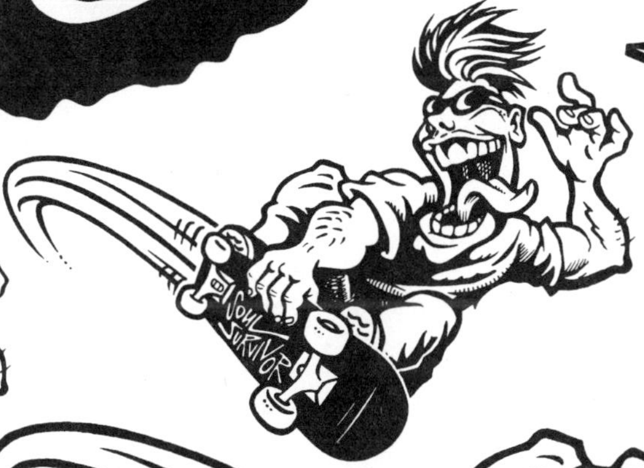

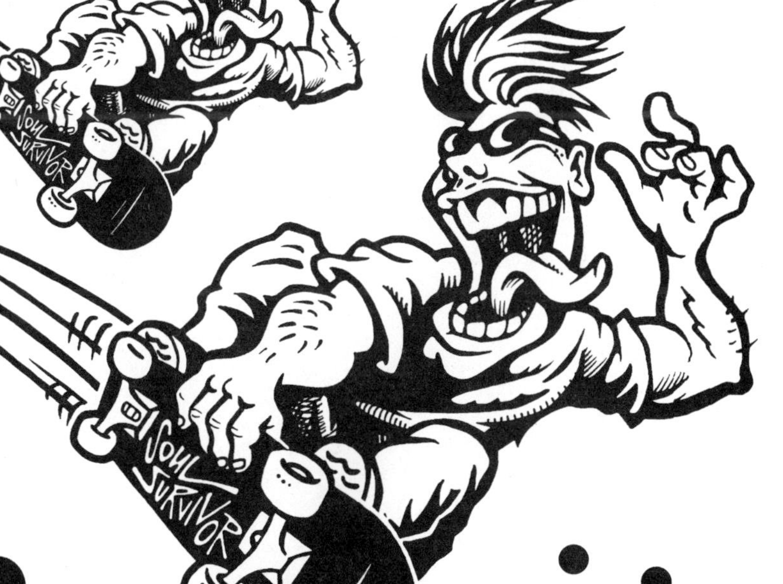

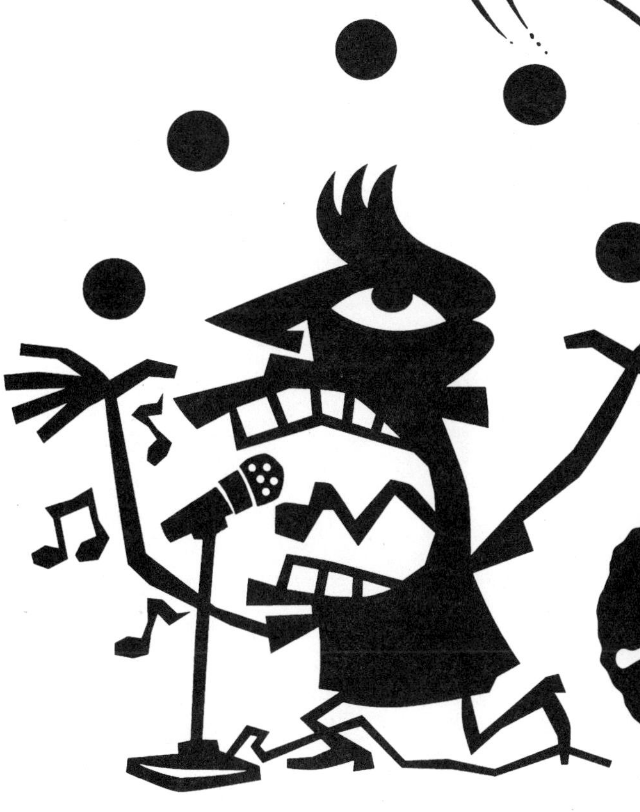

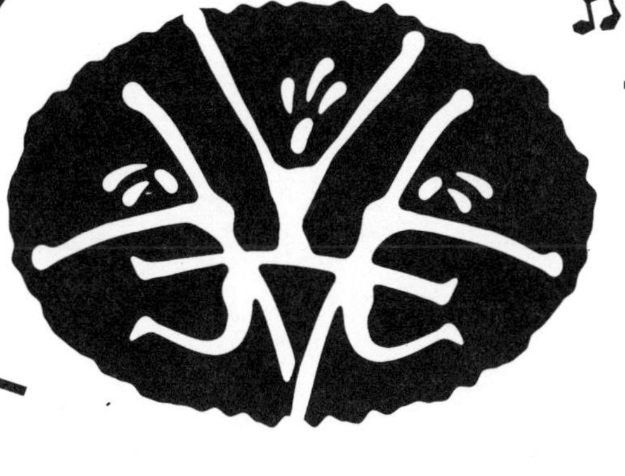

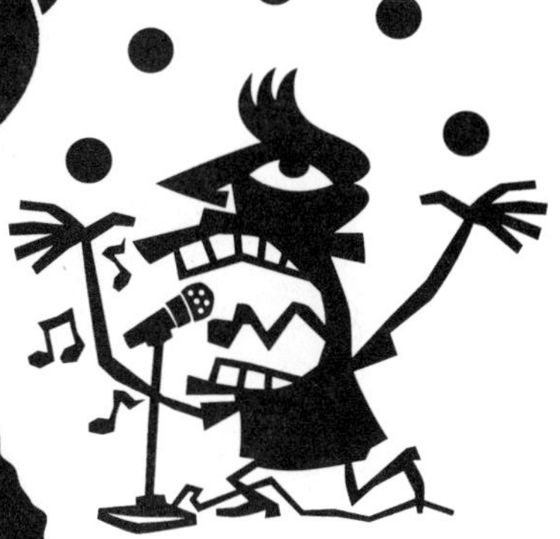

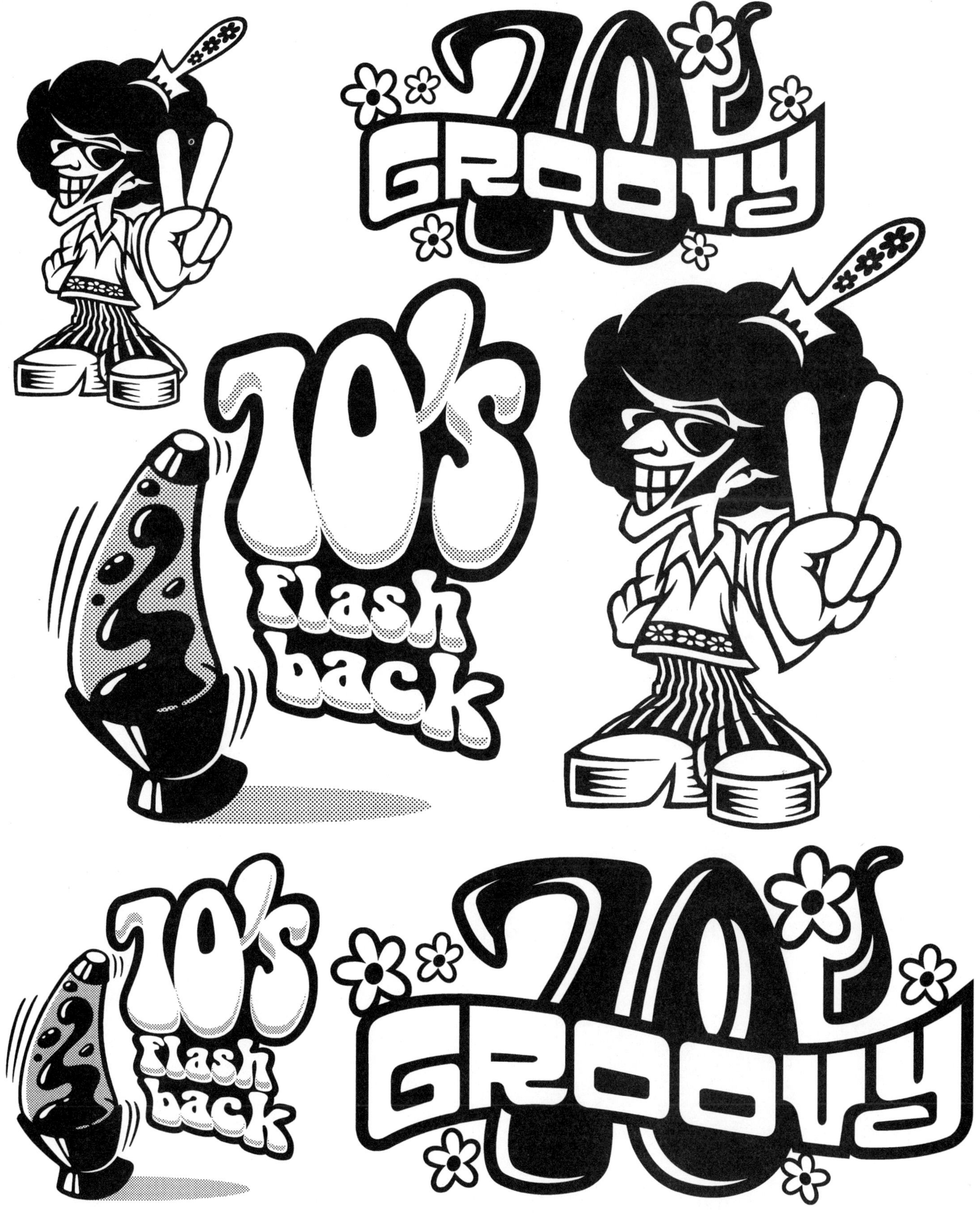
70's
GROOVY
70's
Flash
back
70's
Flash
back
70's
GROOVY

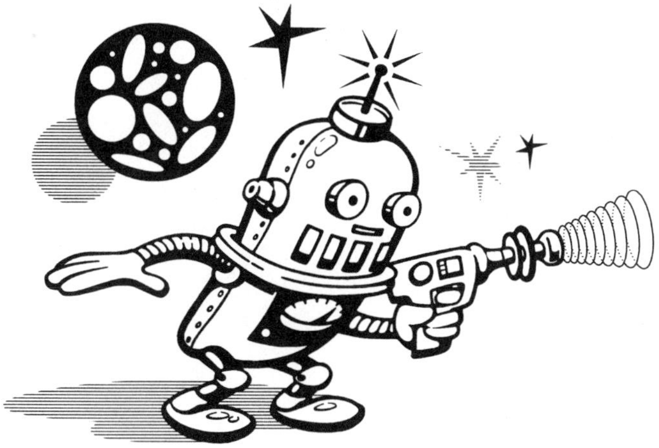

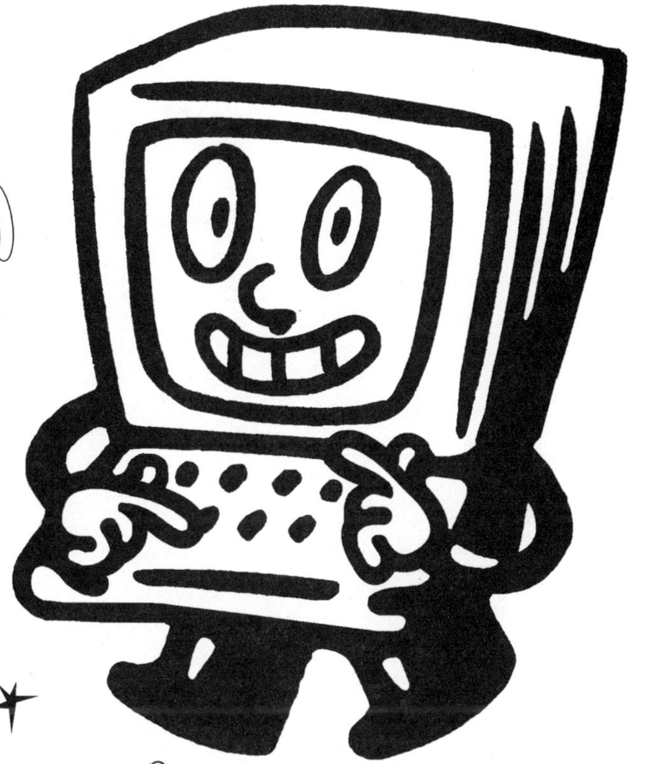

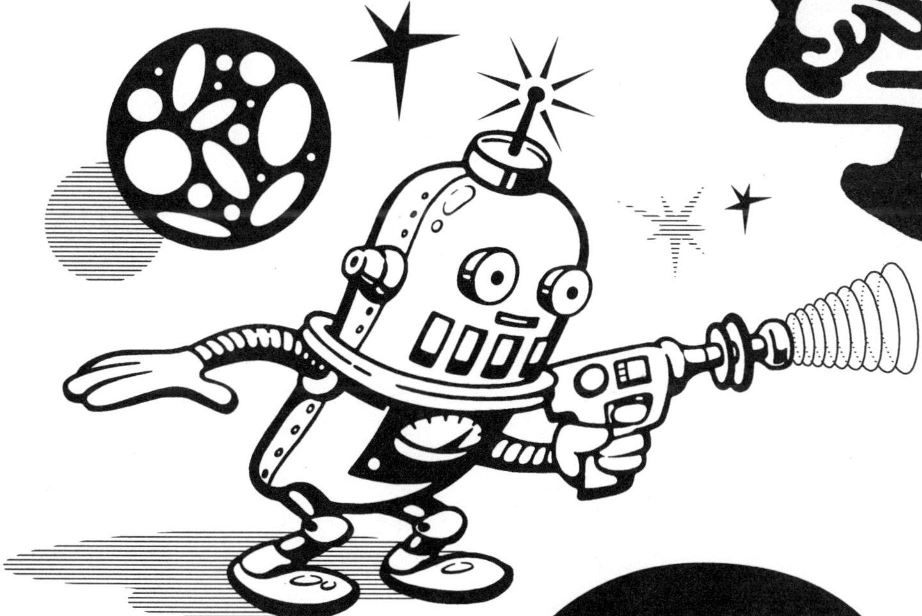

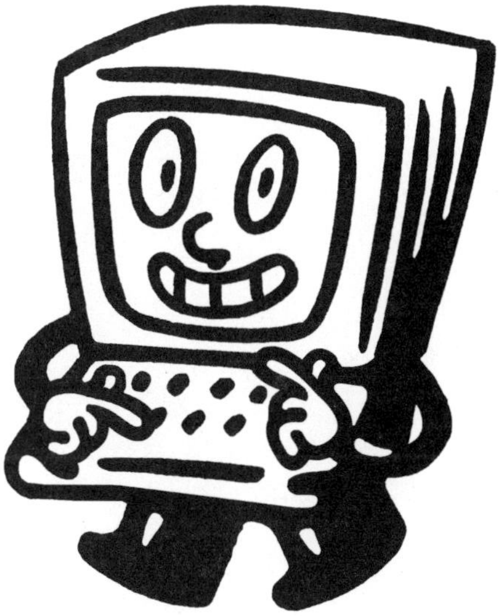

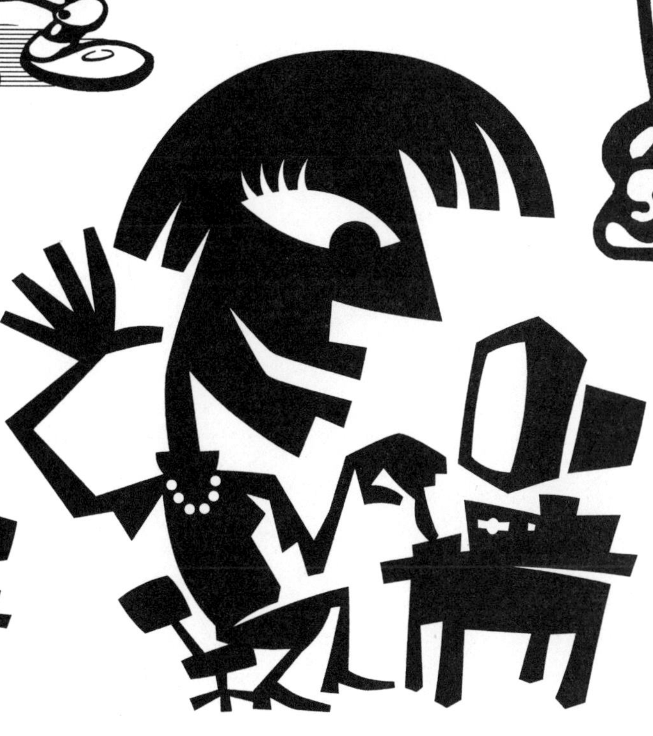

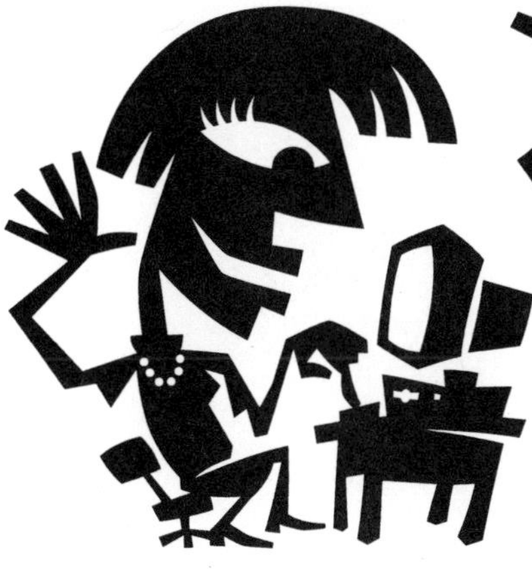

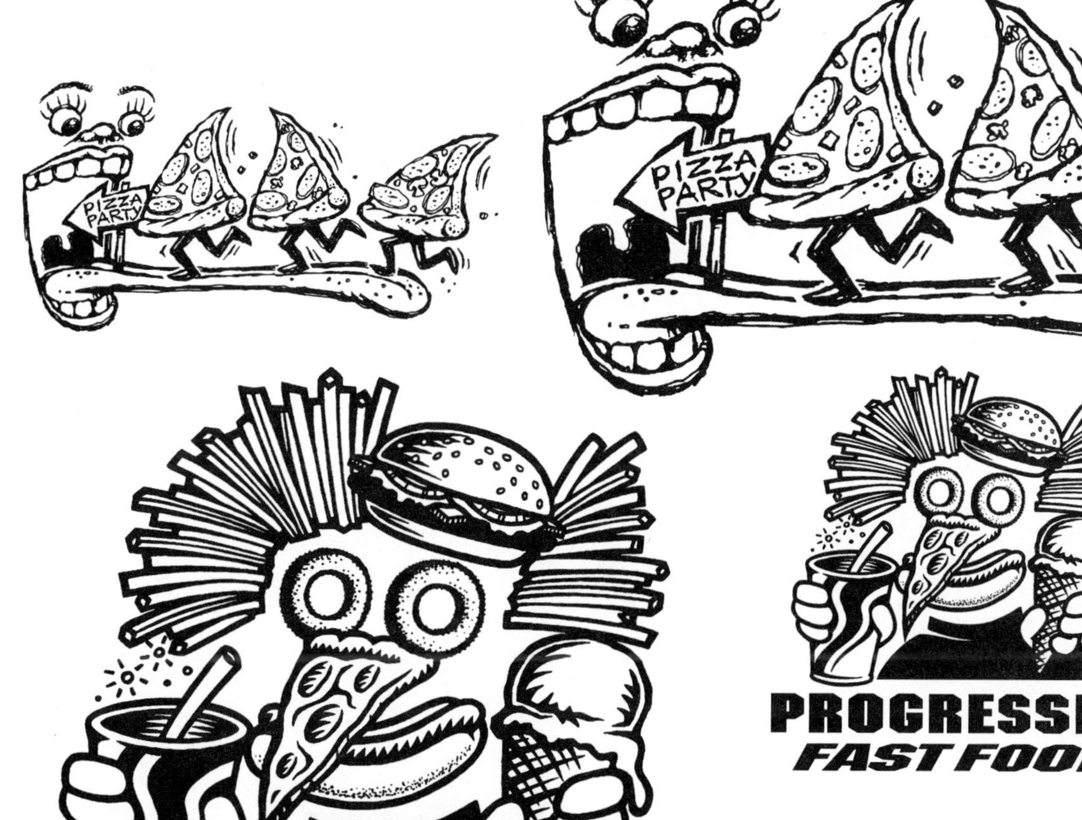

PIZZA PARTY

PROGRESSIVE
FAST FOOD

PROGRESSIVE
FAST FOOD

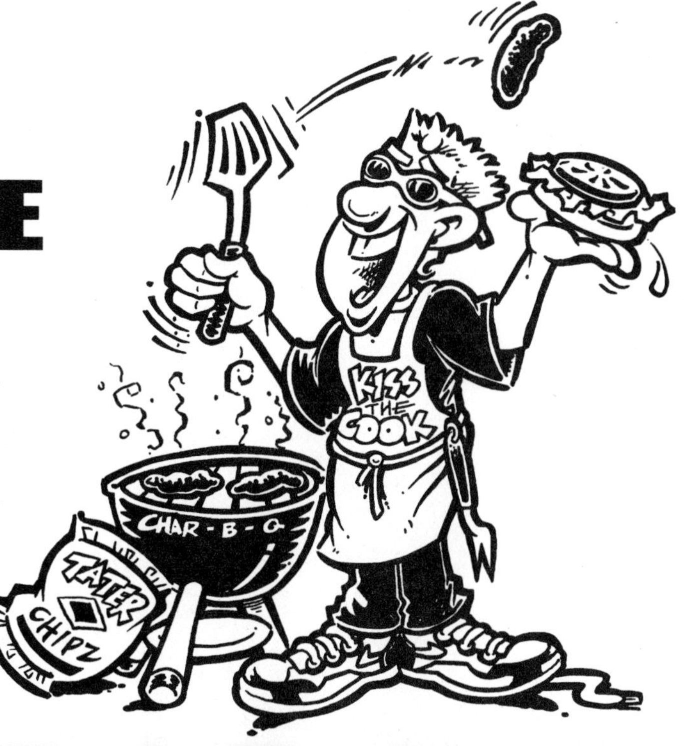

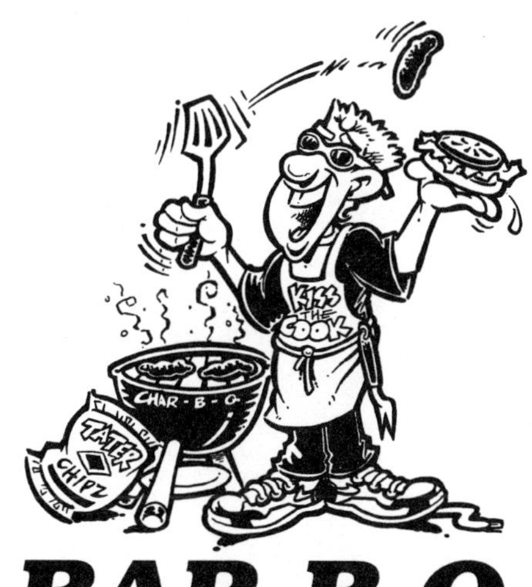

BAR-B-Q

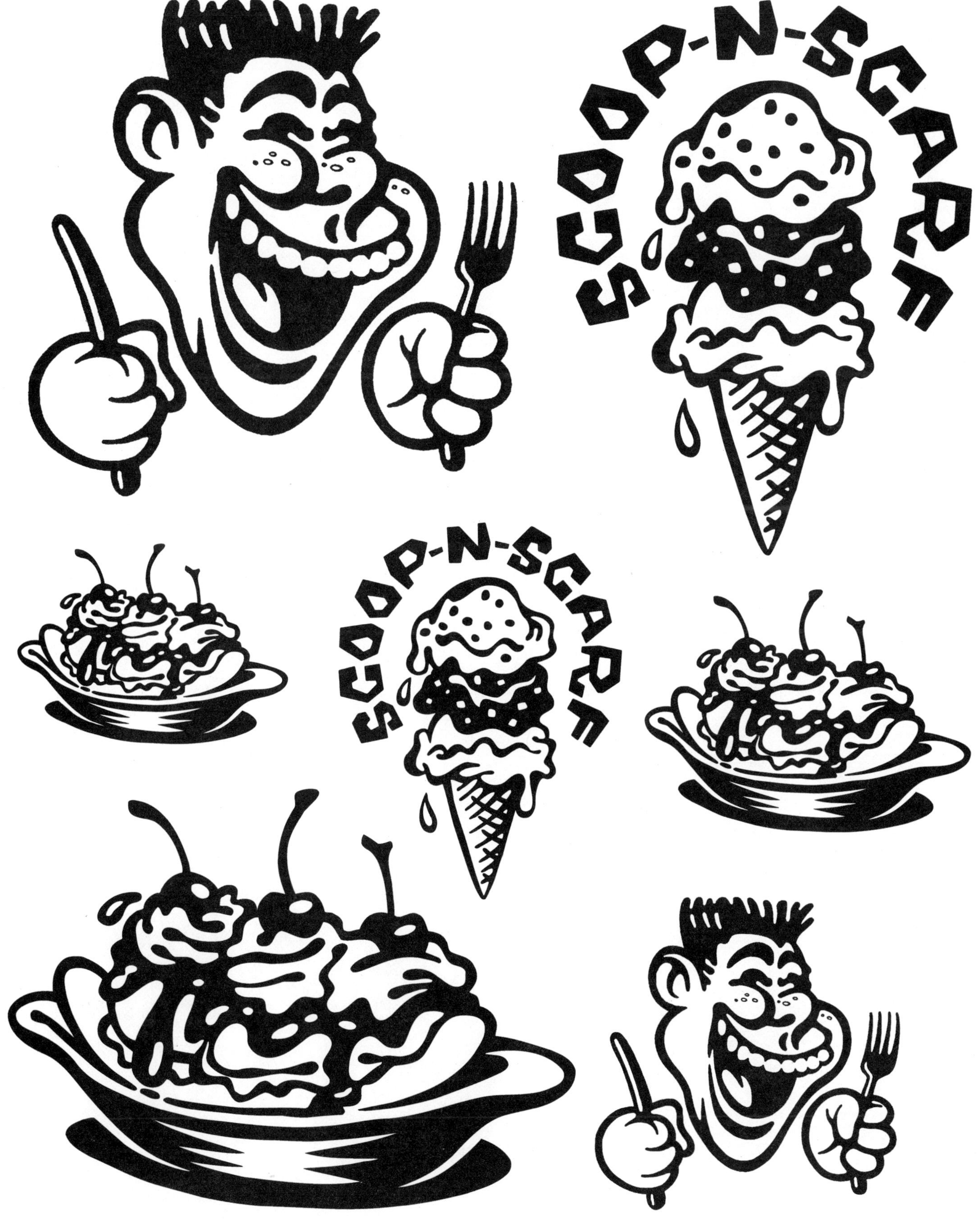
SCOOP-N-SCARF
SCOOP-N-SCARF

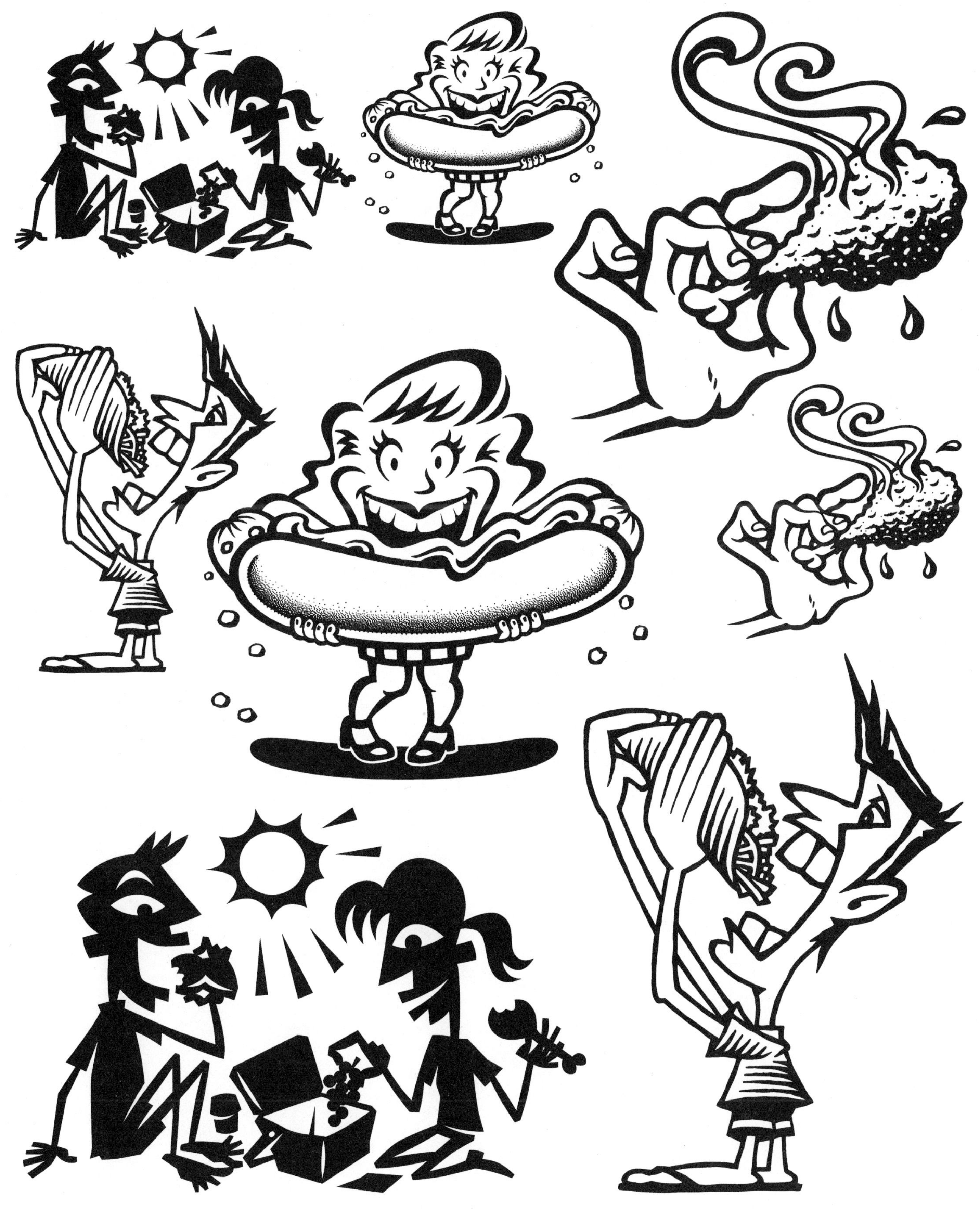

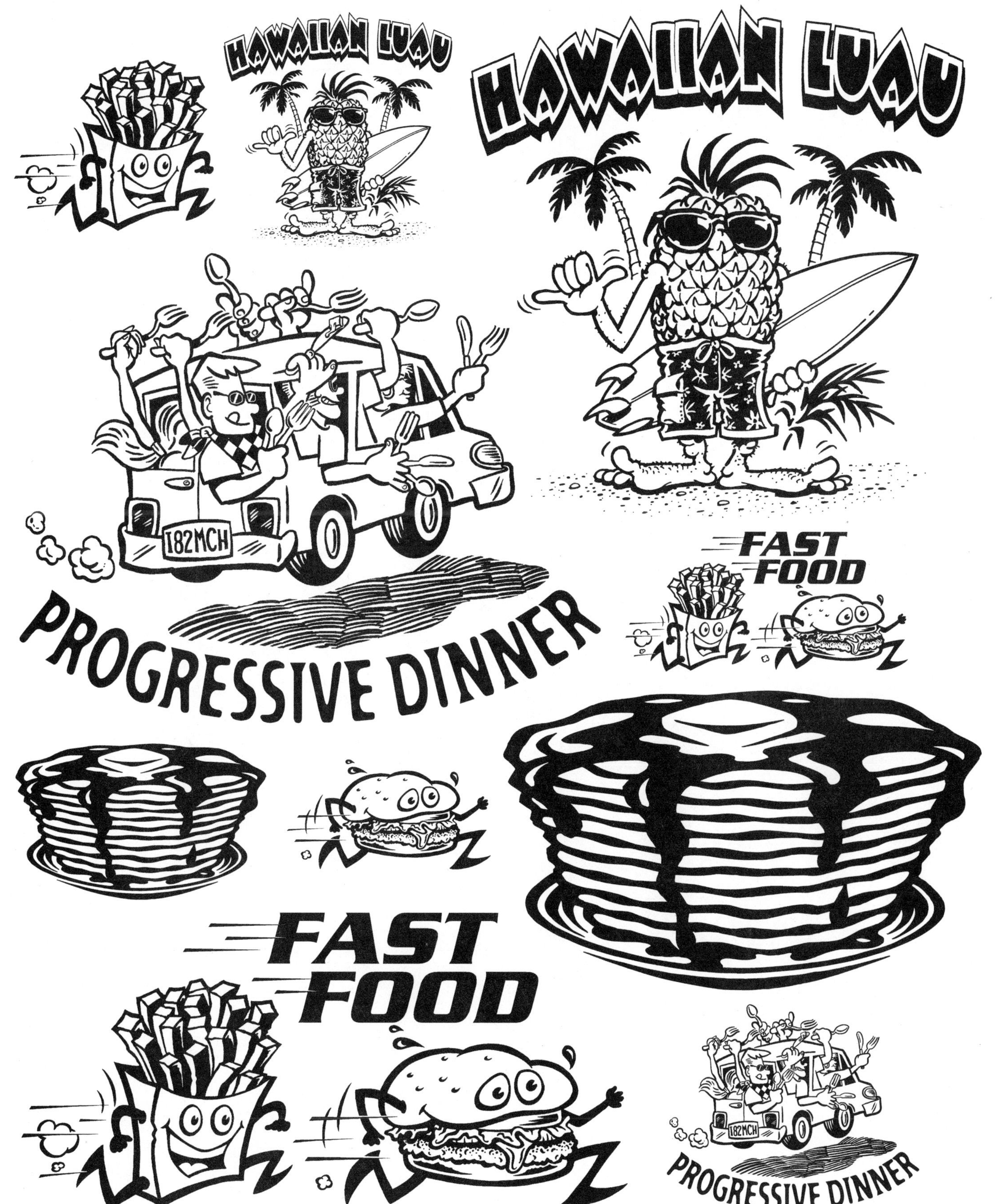
HAWAIIAN LUAU
HAWAIIAN LUAU
182MCH
PROGRESSIVE DINNER
FAST FOOD
FAST FOOD
182MCH
PROGRESSIVE DINNER

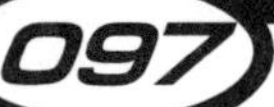
097

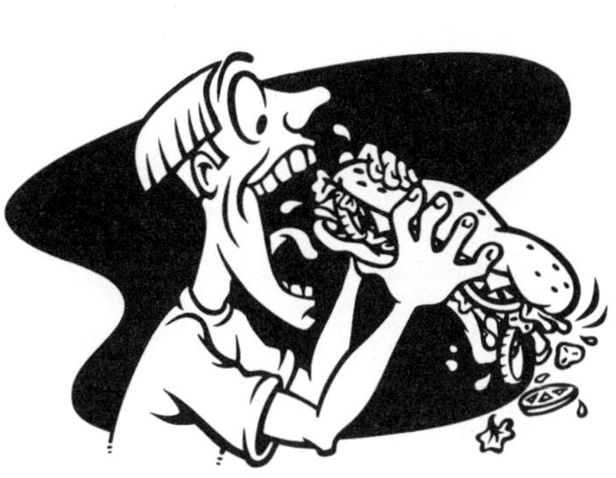

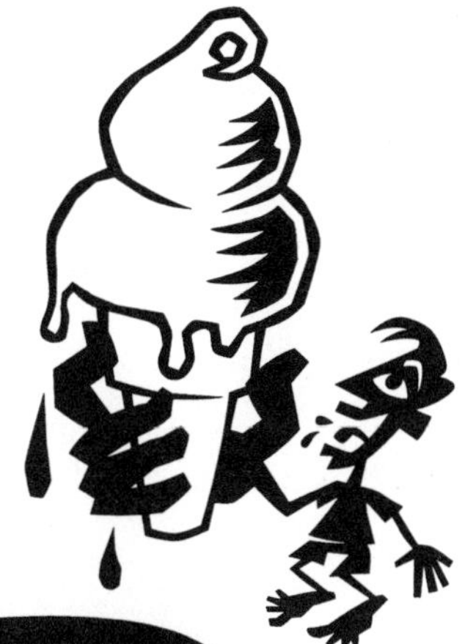

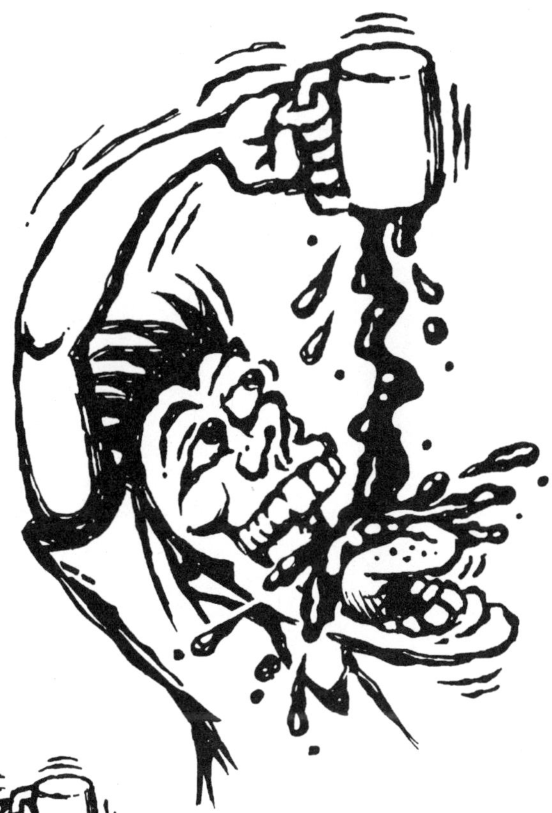

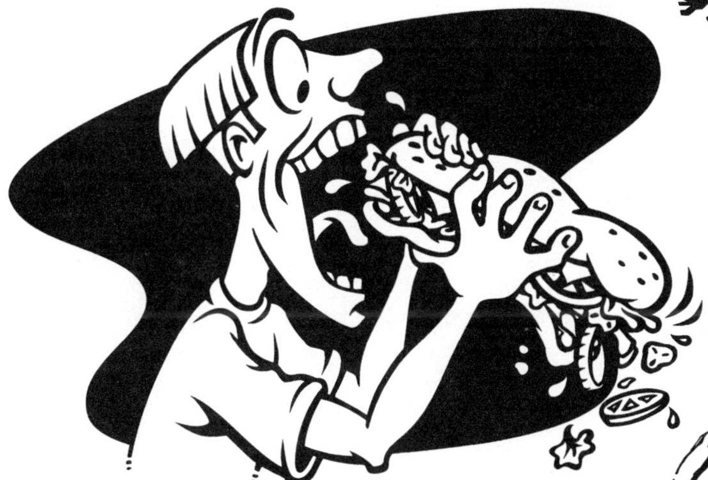

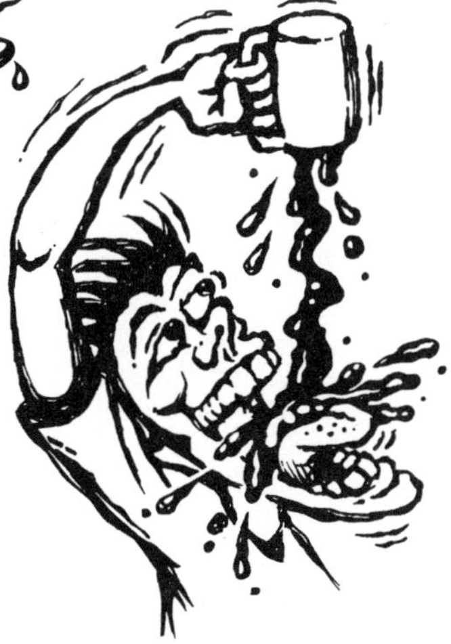

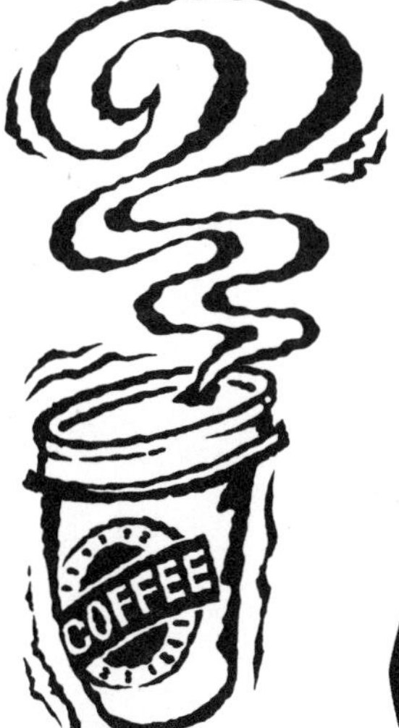

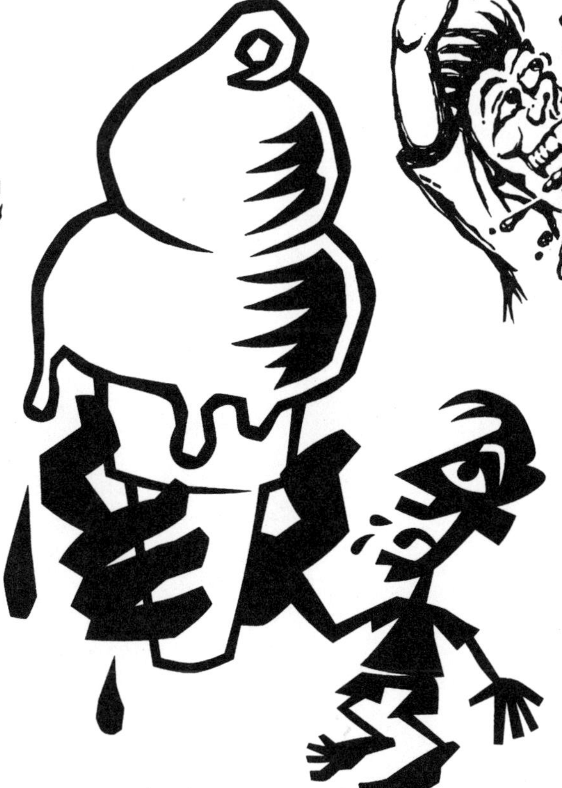

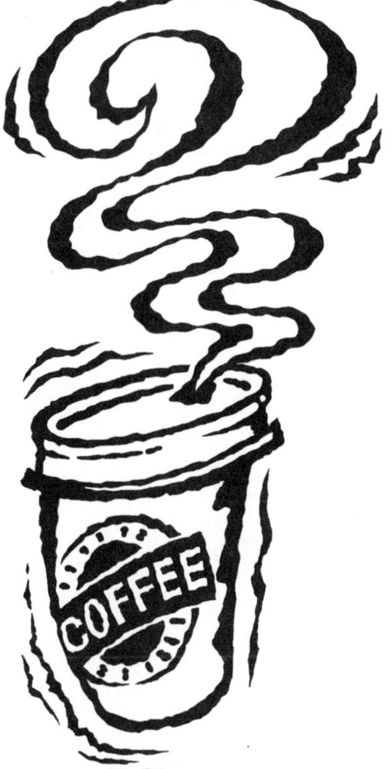

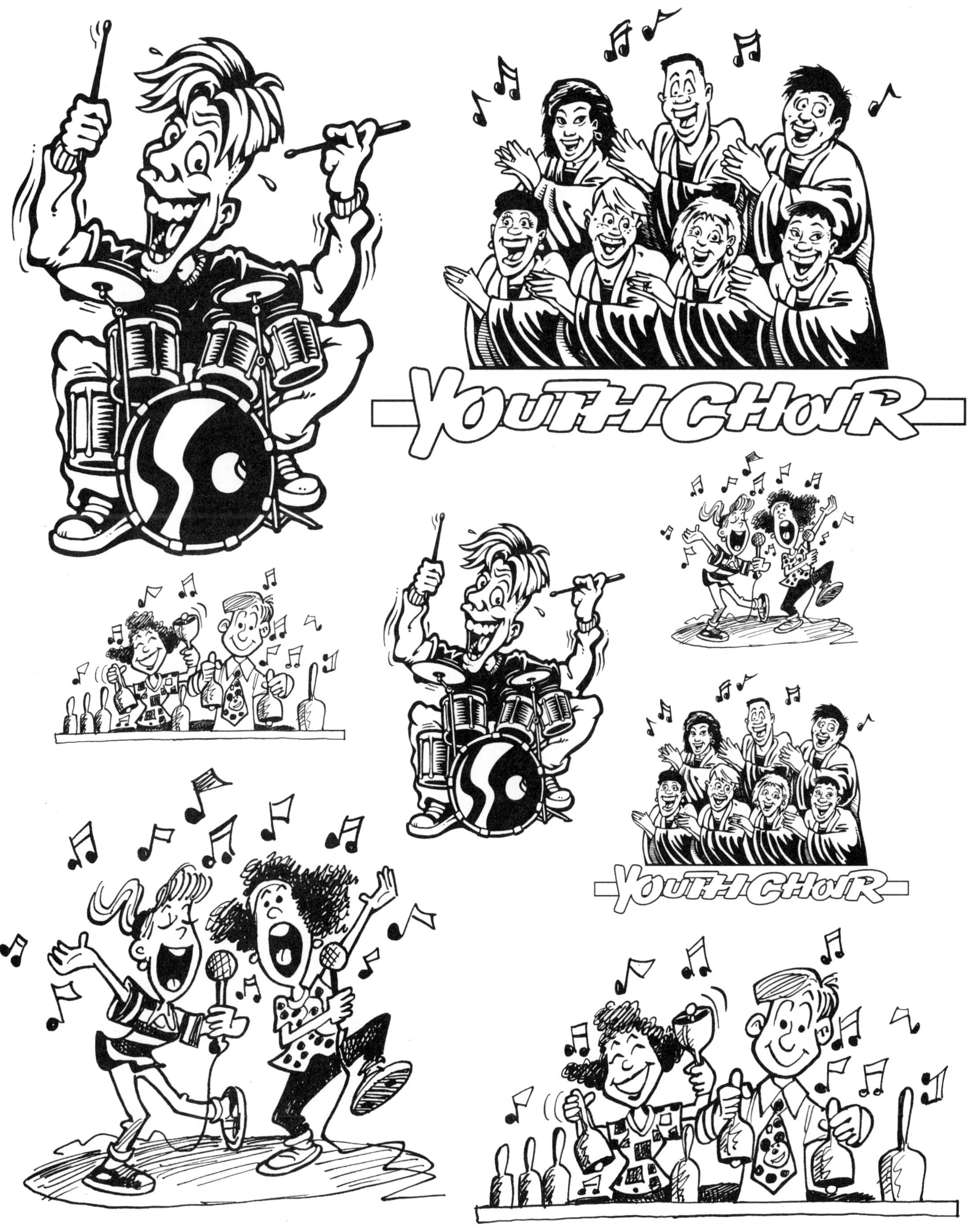
YOUTH CHOIR
YOUTH CHOIR

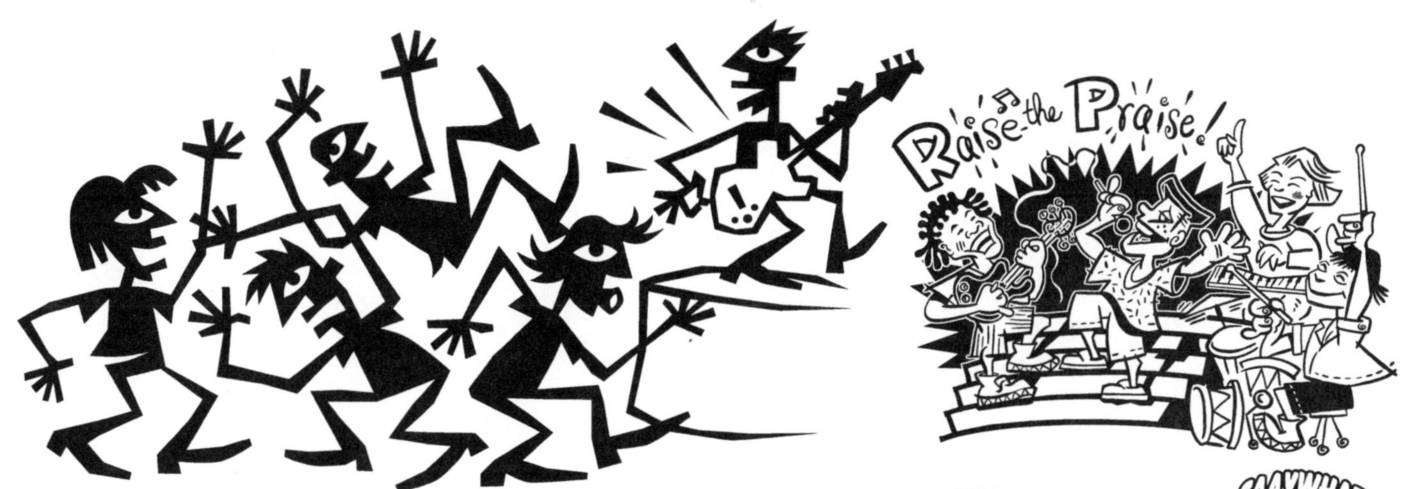
Raise the Praise!

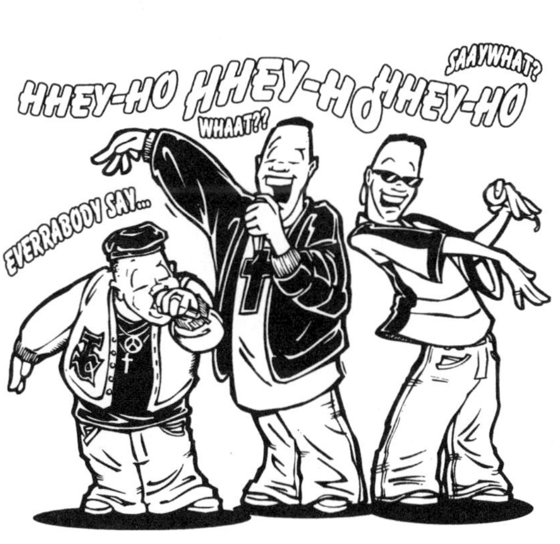
HHEY-HO HHEY-HO HHEY-HO
SAAYWHAT?
WHAAT??
EVERRABODY SAY...

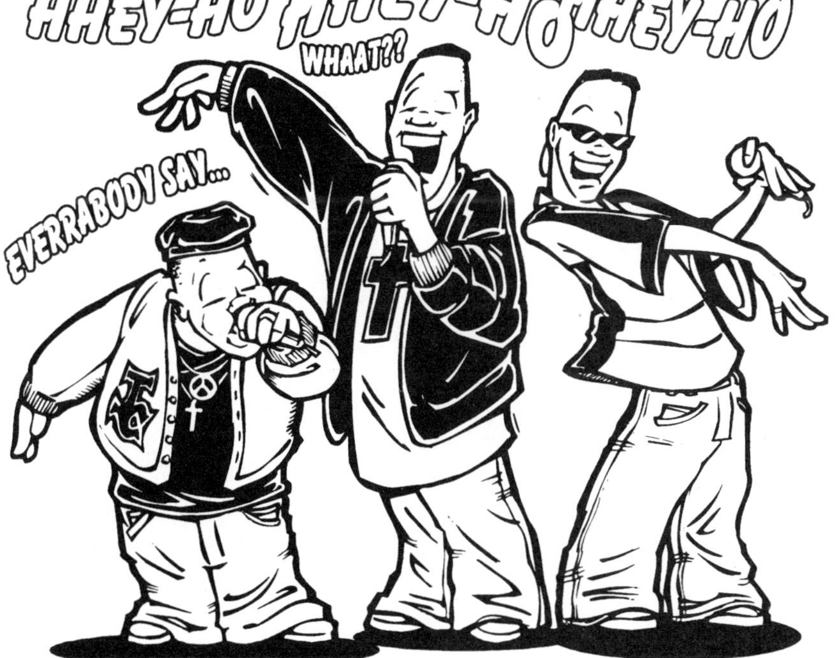
HHEY-HO HHEY-HO HHEY-HO
SAAYWHAT?
WHAAT??
EVERRABODY SAY...

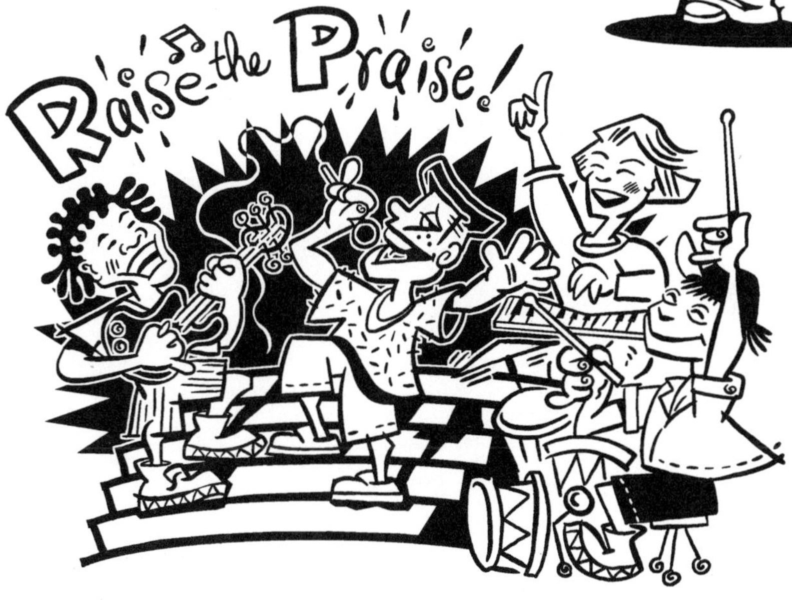
Raise the Praise!

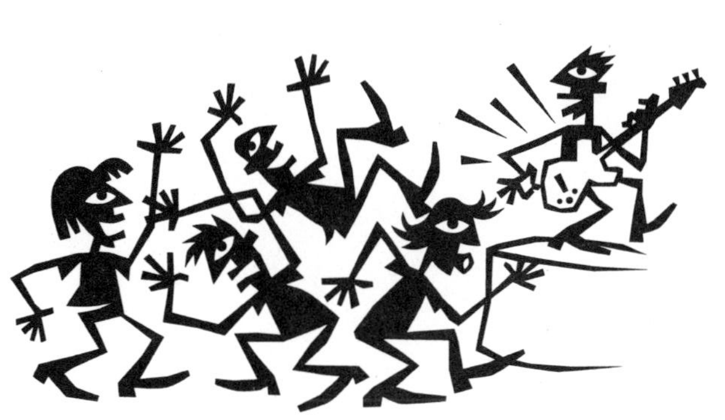

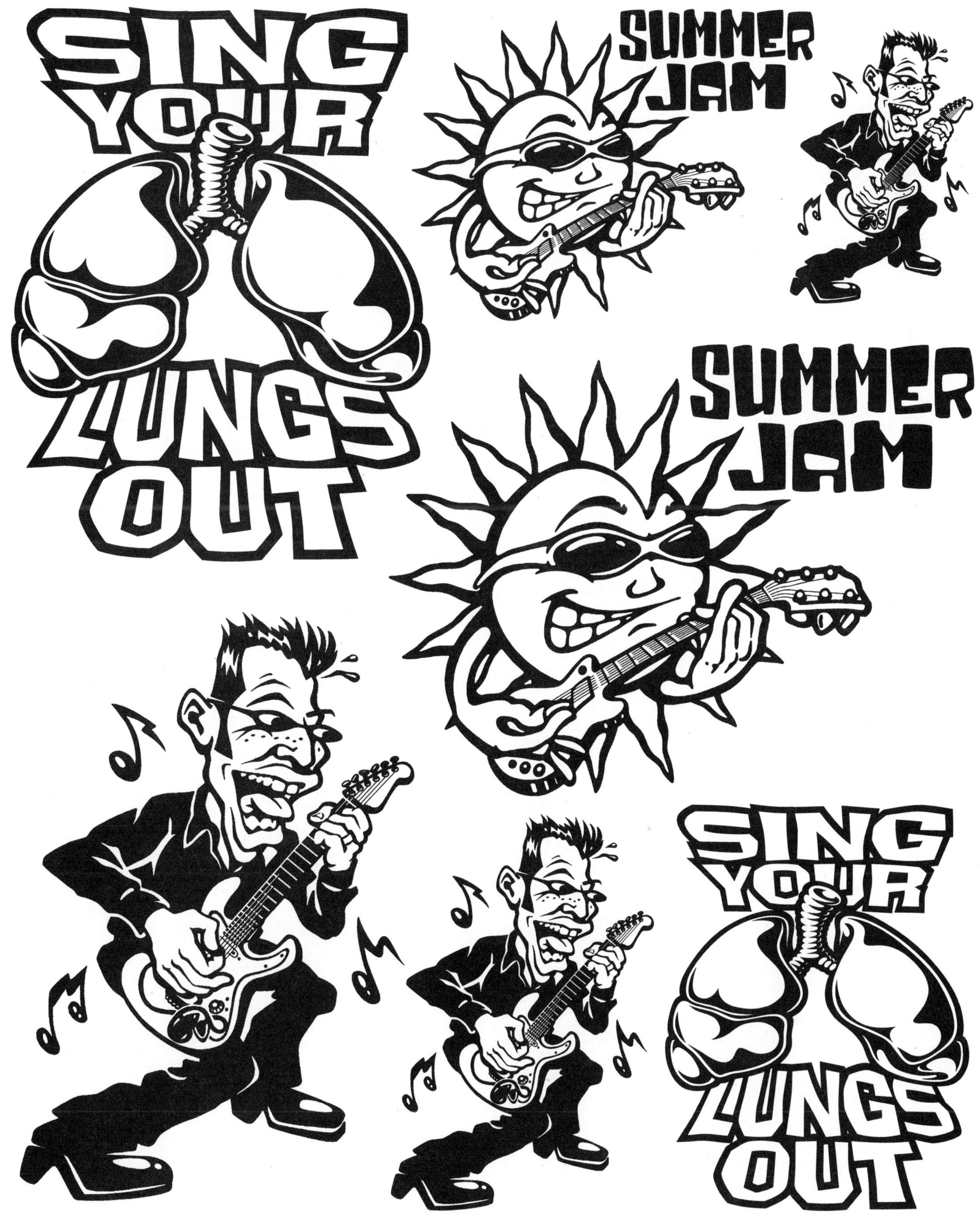
SING YOUR LUNGS OUT
SUMMER JAM
SUMMER JAM
SING YOUR LUNGS OUT

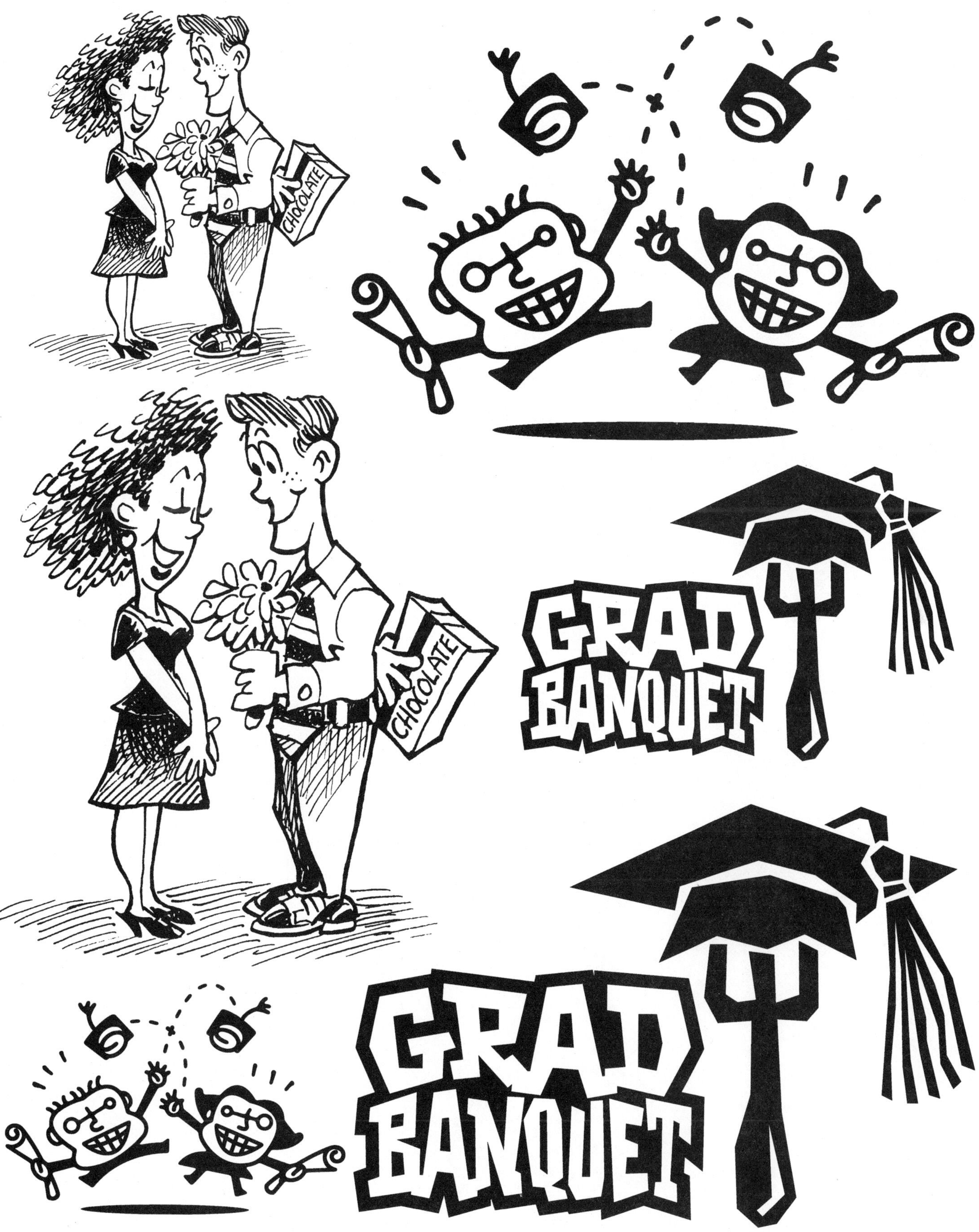
CHOCOLATE
CHOCOLATE
GRAD BANQUET
GRAD BANQUET

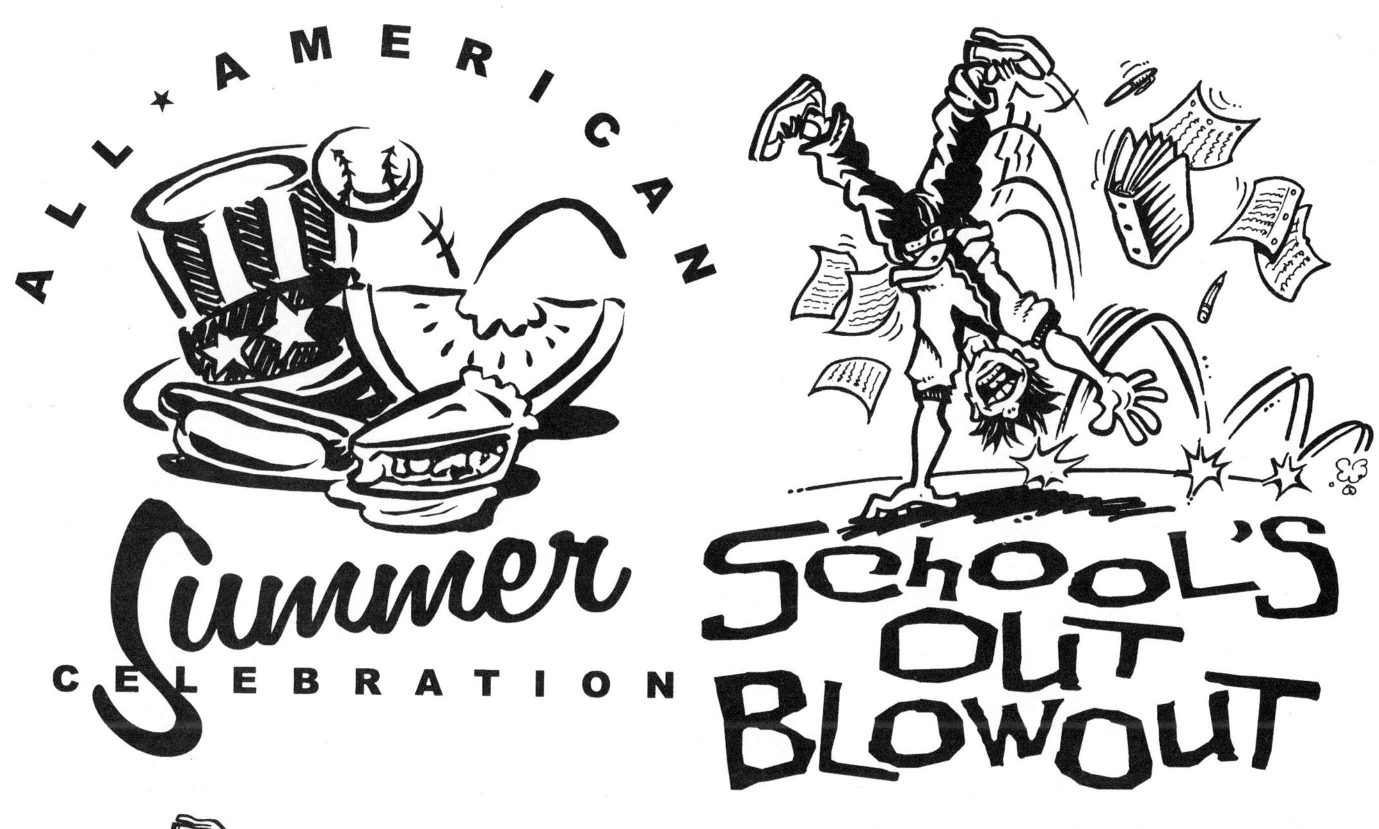

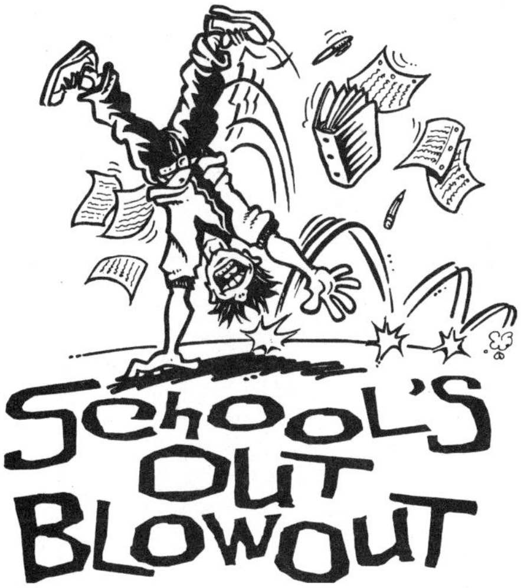

SCHOOL'S
OUT
BLOWOUT

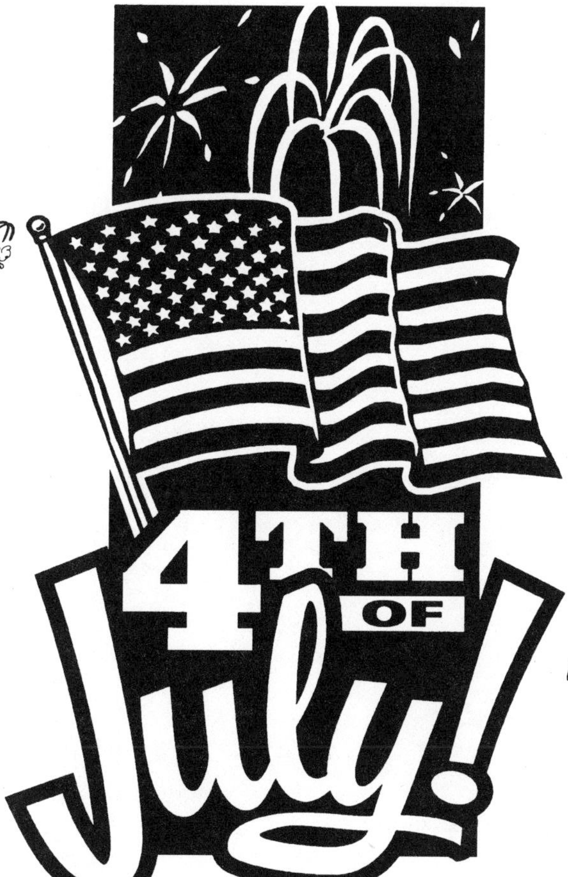

4TH OF
July!

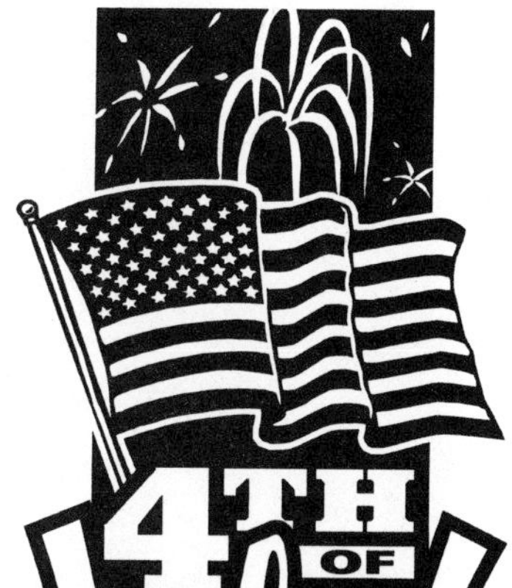

4TH OF
July!

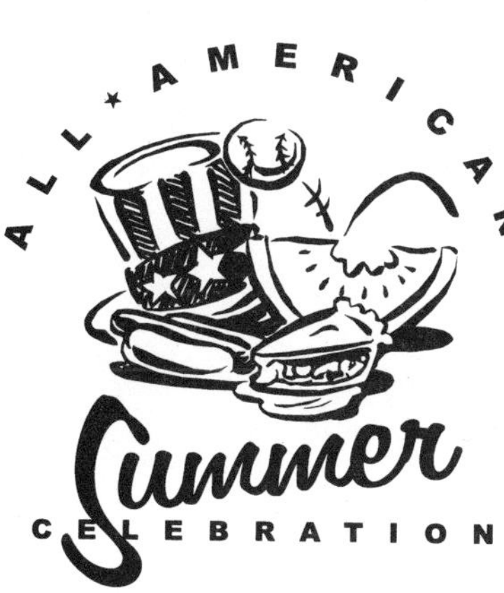

ALL ★ AMERICAN
Summer
CELEBRATION

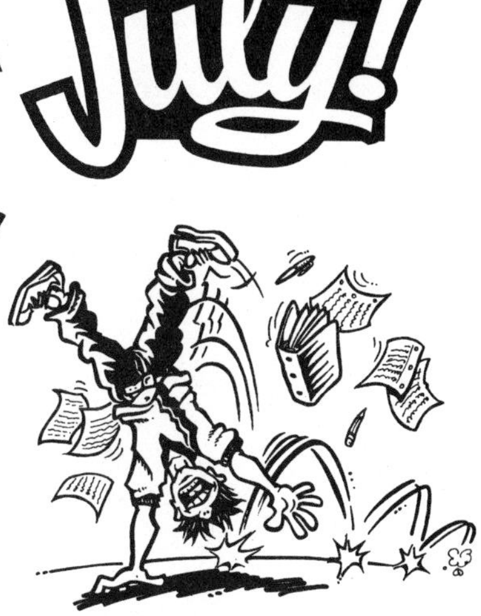

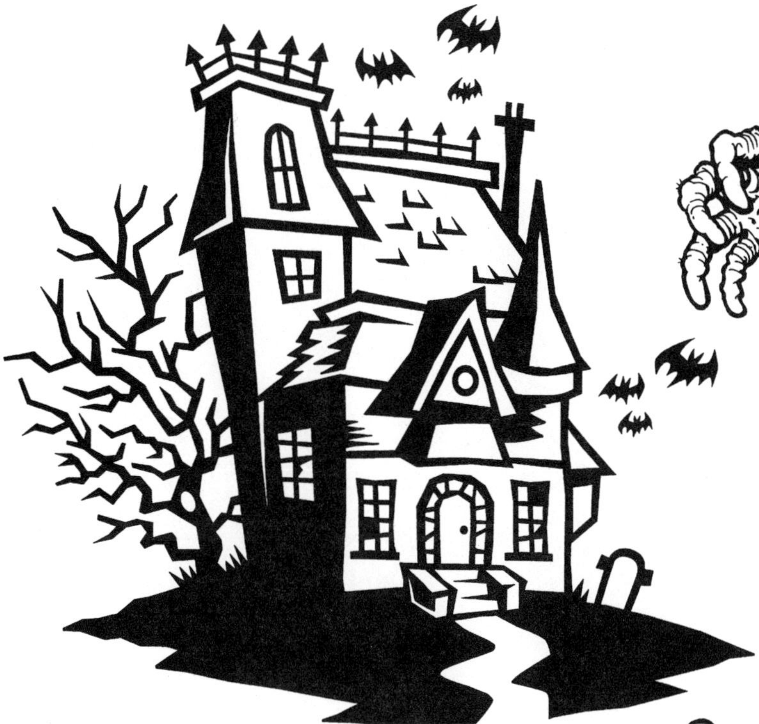

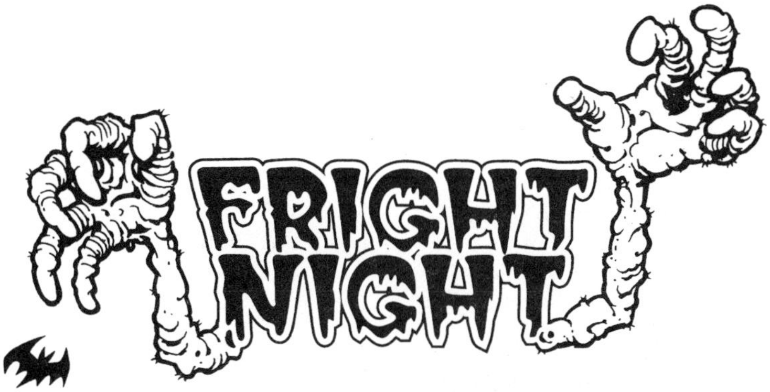

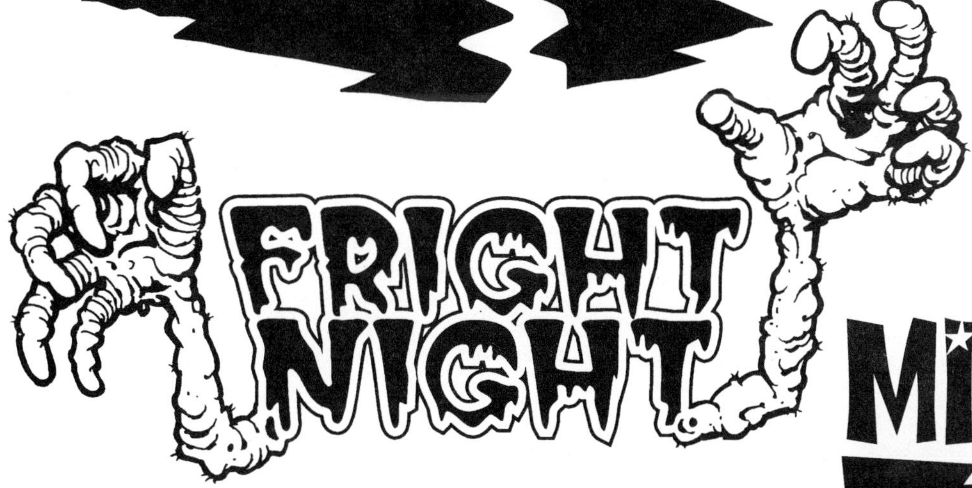

FRIGHT NIGHT

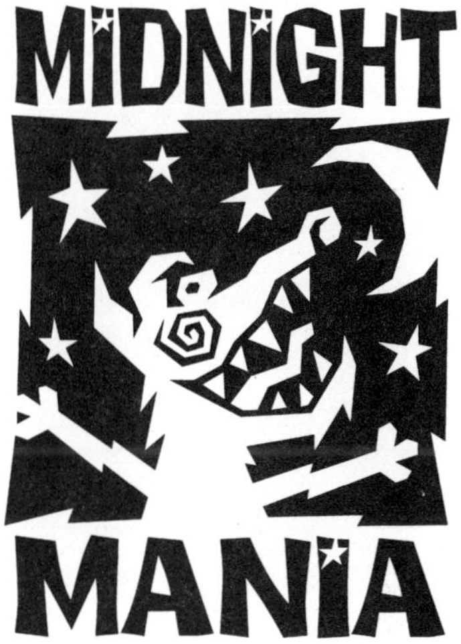

MIDNIGHT MANIA

FRIGHT NIGHT

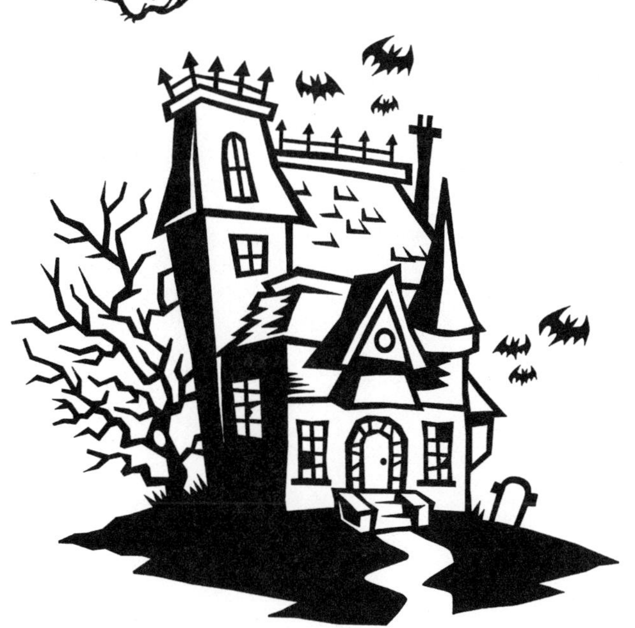

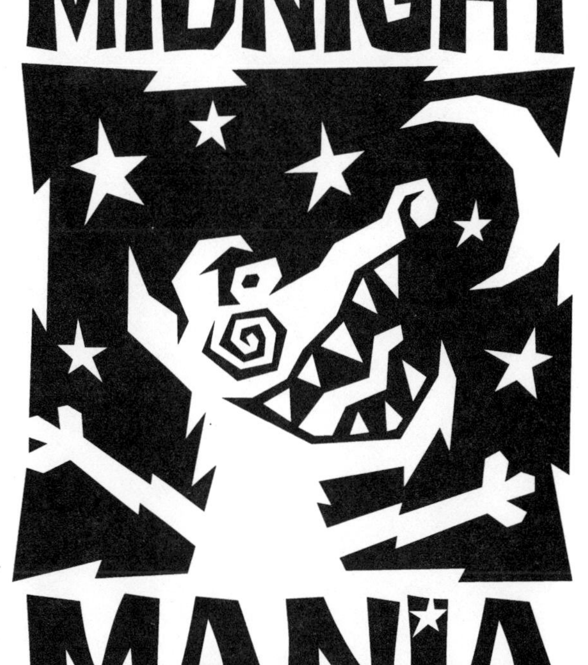

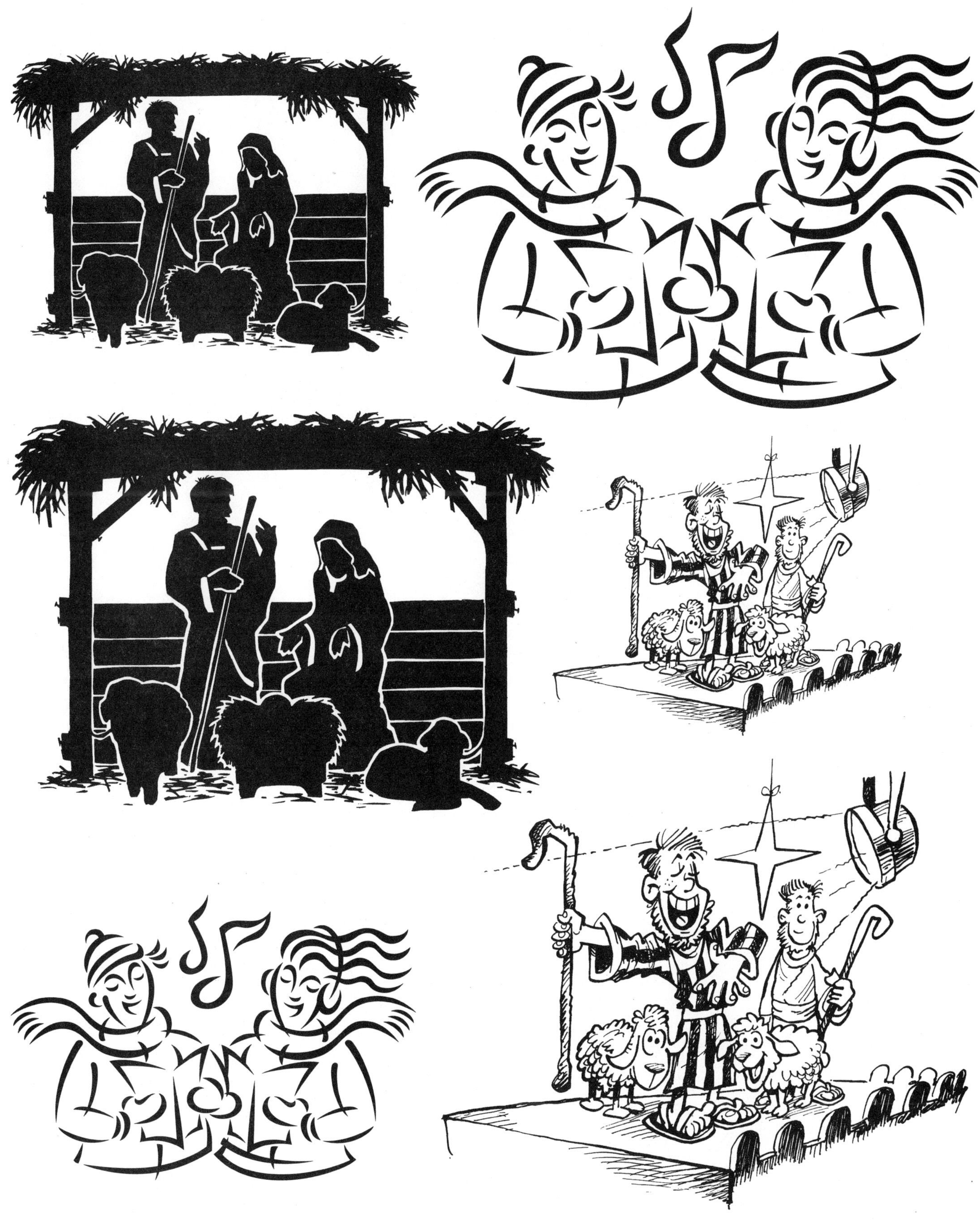

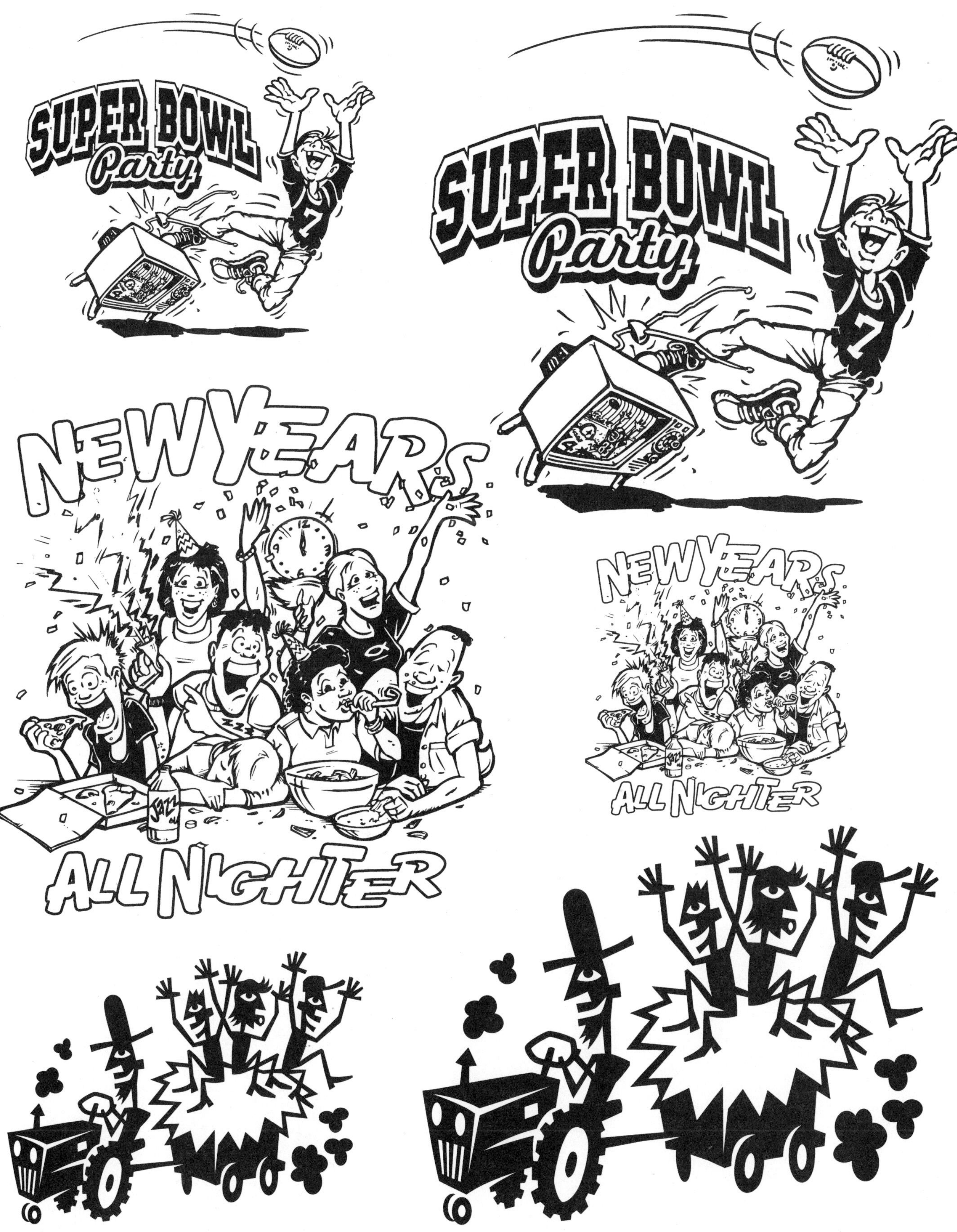
SUPER BOWL
Party
7
SUPER BOWL
Party
7
NEW YEARS
ALL NIGHTER
NEW YEARS
ALL NIGHTER

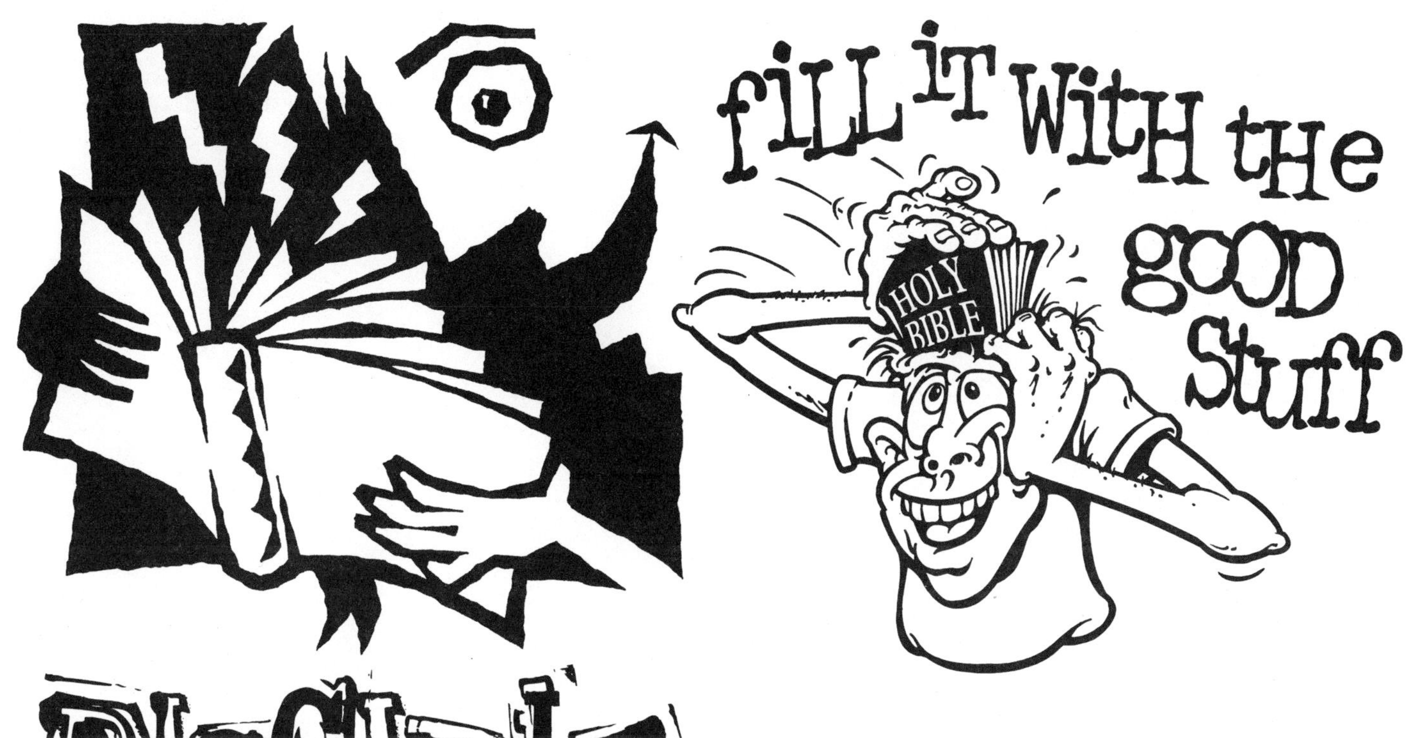
fill it with the good Stuff
HOLY BIBLE

DISCIPLE NOW

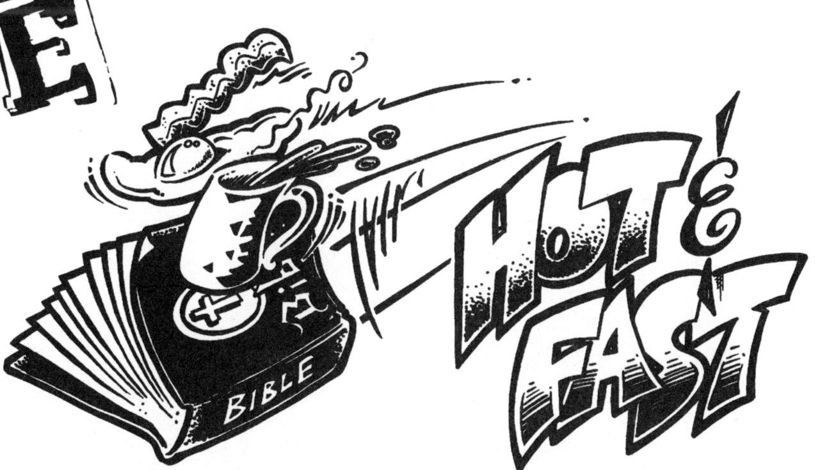
BIBLE
HOT & FAST
BREAKFAST CLUB

DISCIPLE NOW

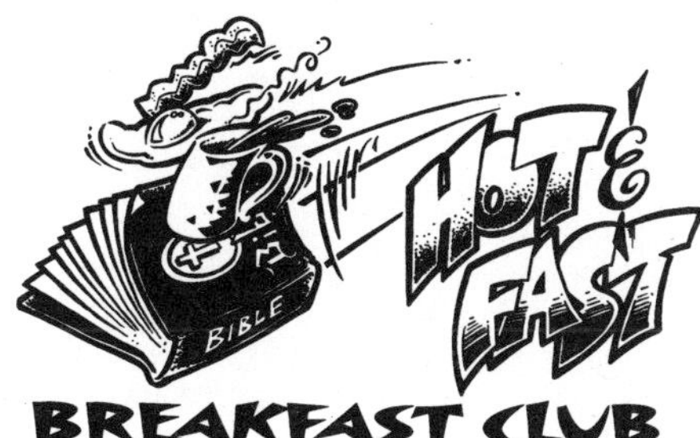
BIBLE
HOT & FAST
BREAKFAST CLUB

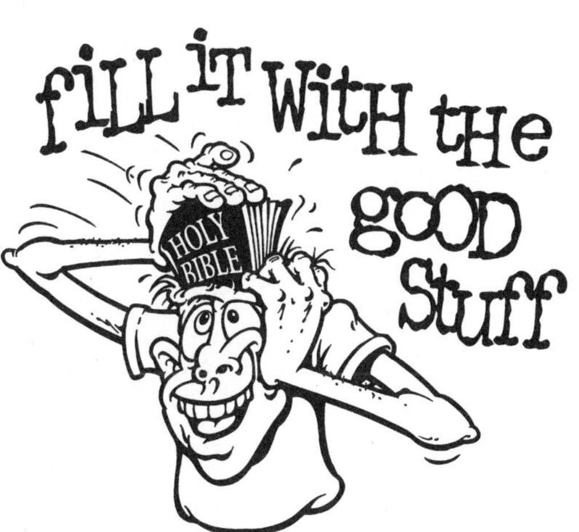
fill it with the good Stuff
HOLY BIBLE

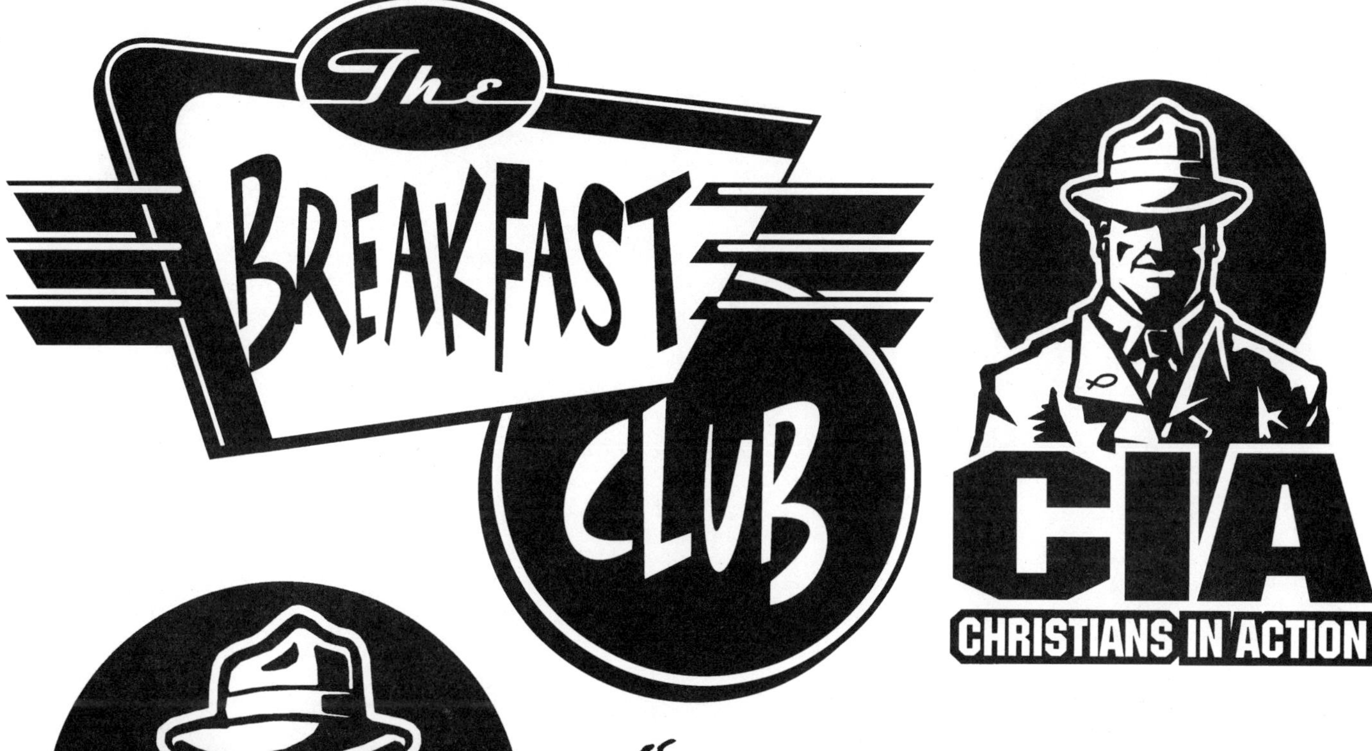

CIA
CHRISTIANS IN ACTION

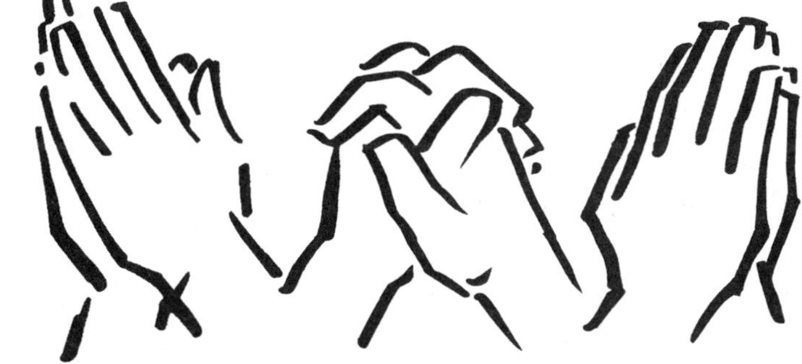

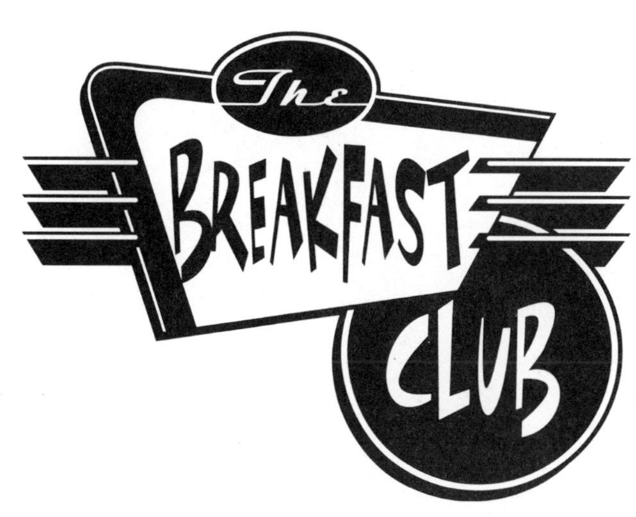

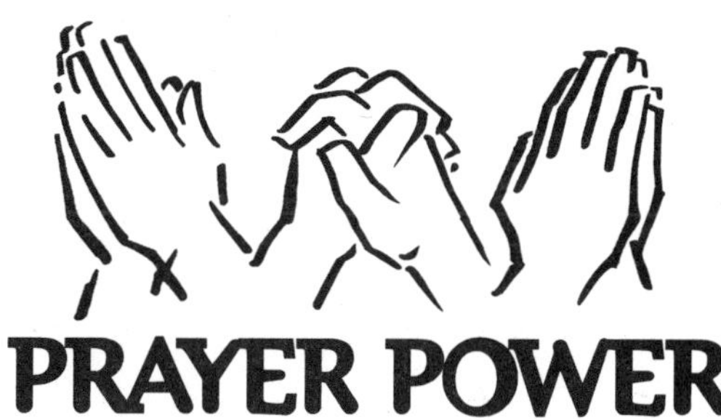

one ON one

PUPPET MINISTRY

one ON one

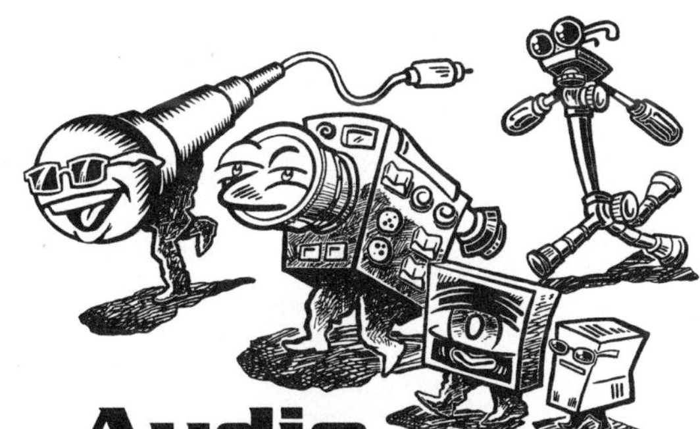

Audio Visual Team

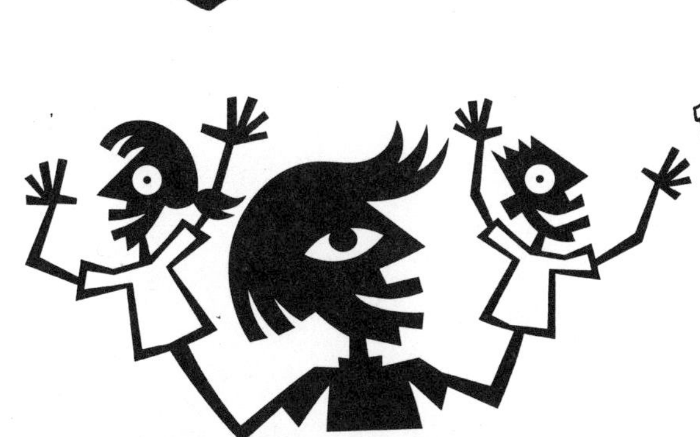

Audio Visual Team

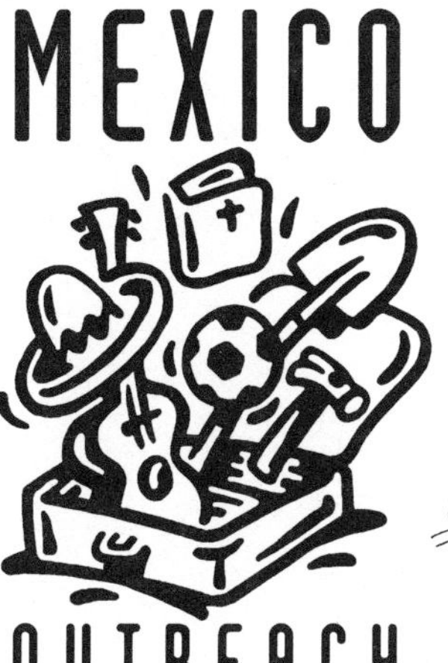

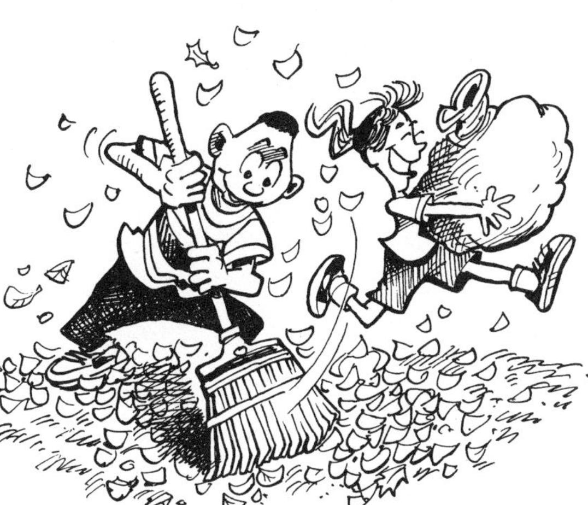

MEXICO

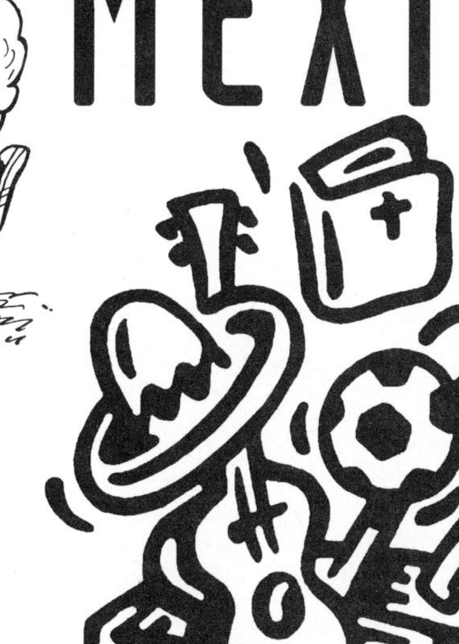

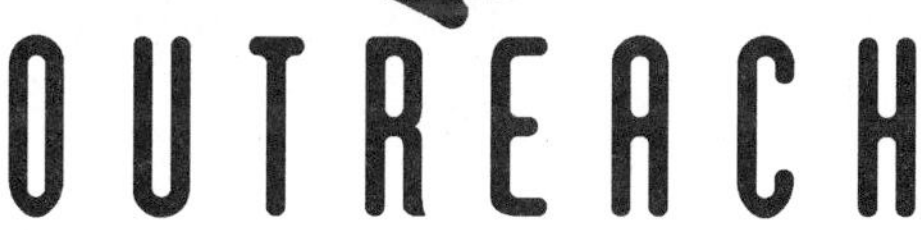

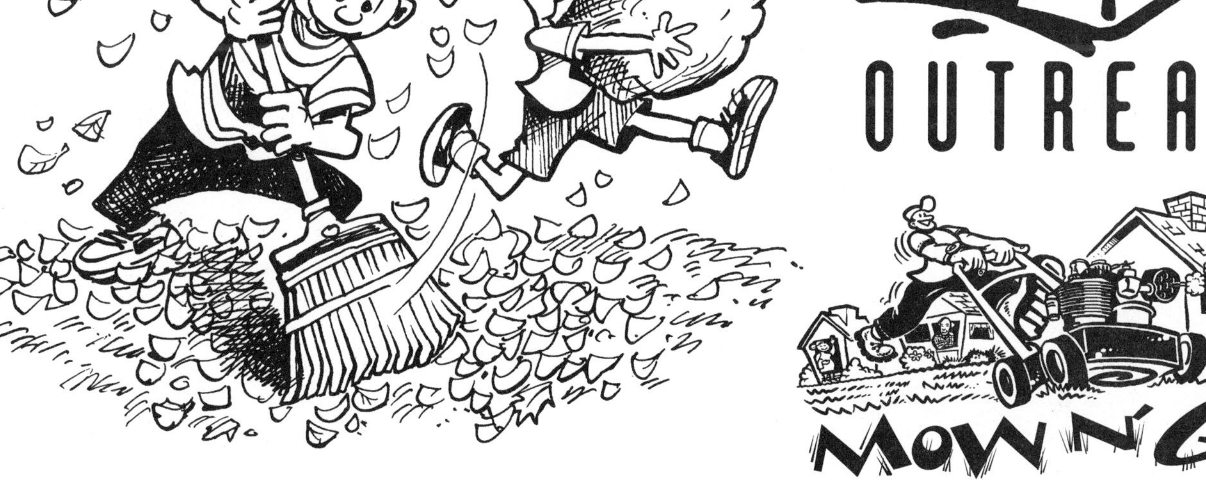

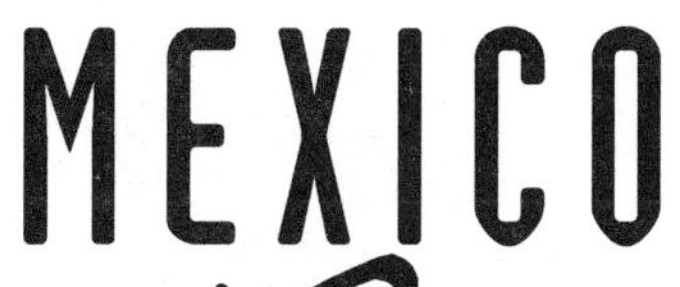

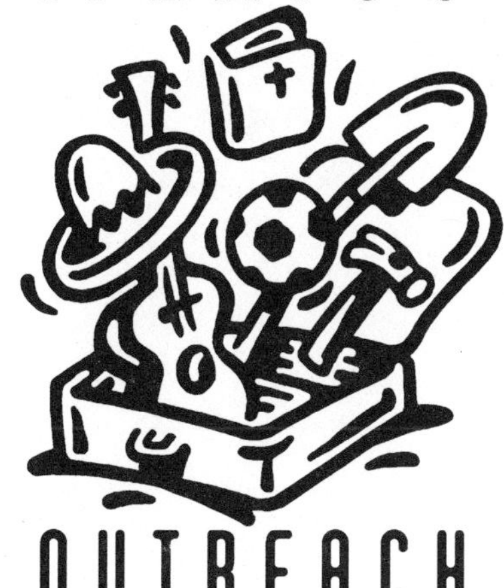

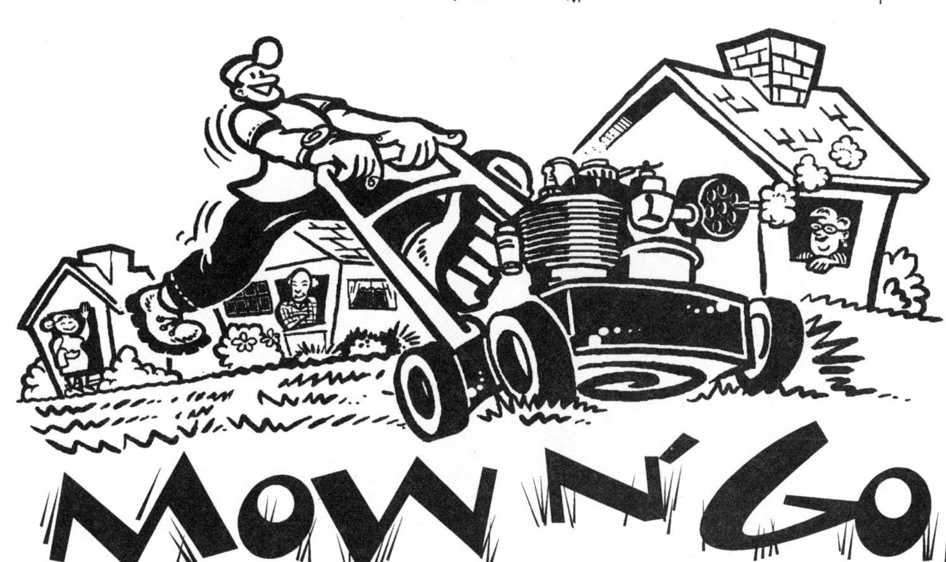

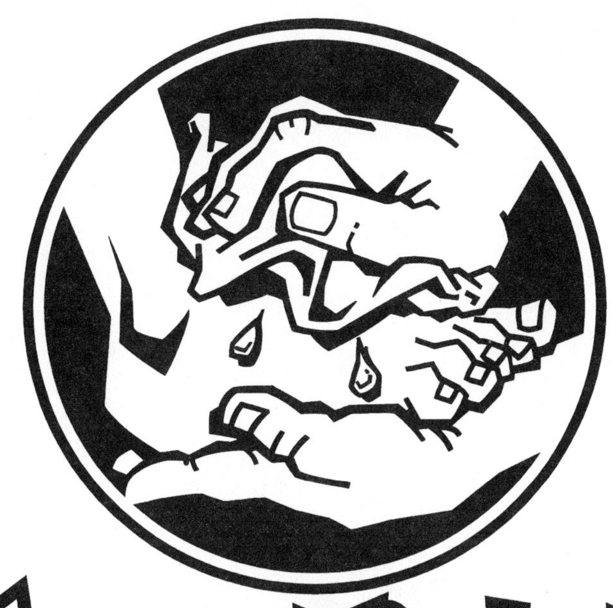

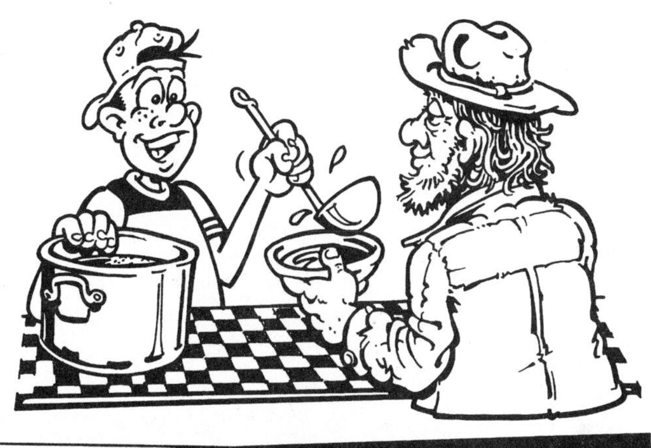

RESCUE MISSION

Servant Project

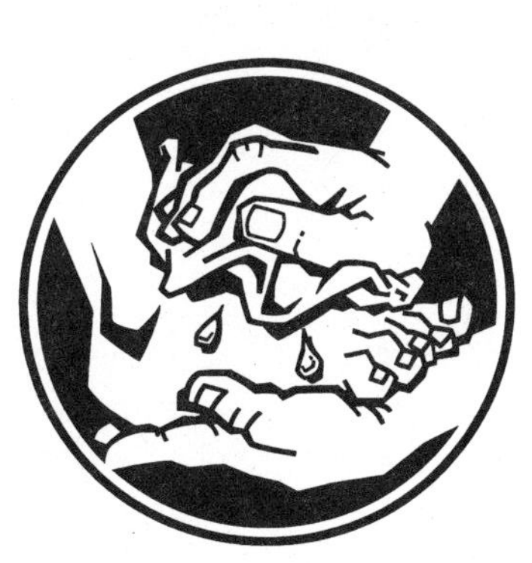

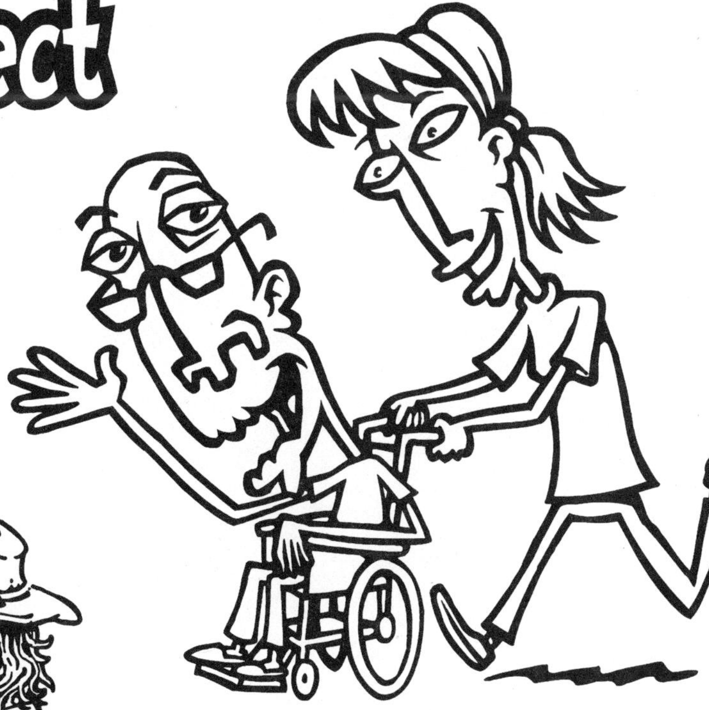

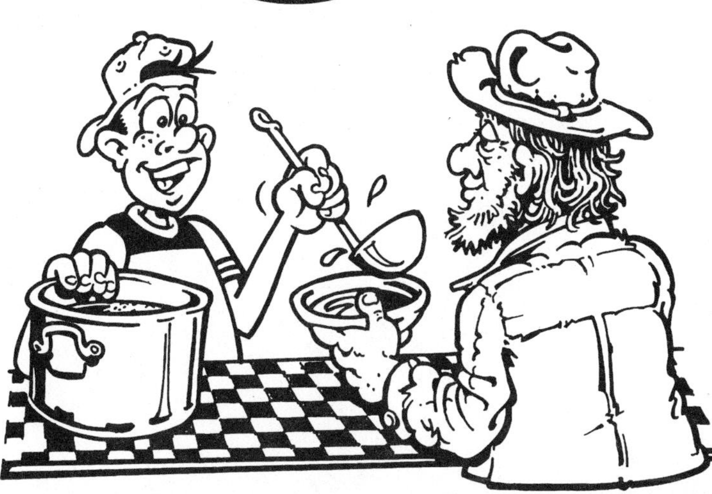

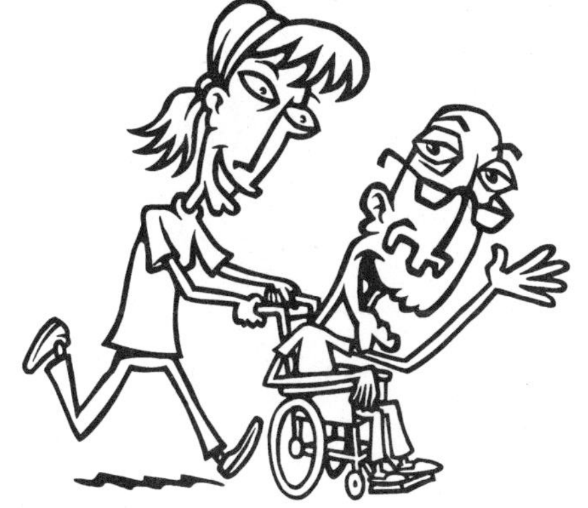

RESCUE MISSION

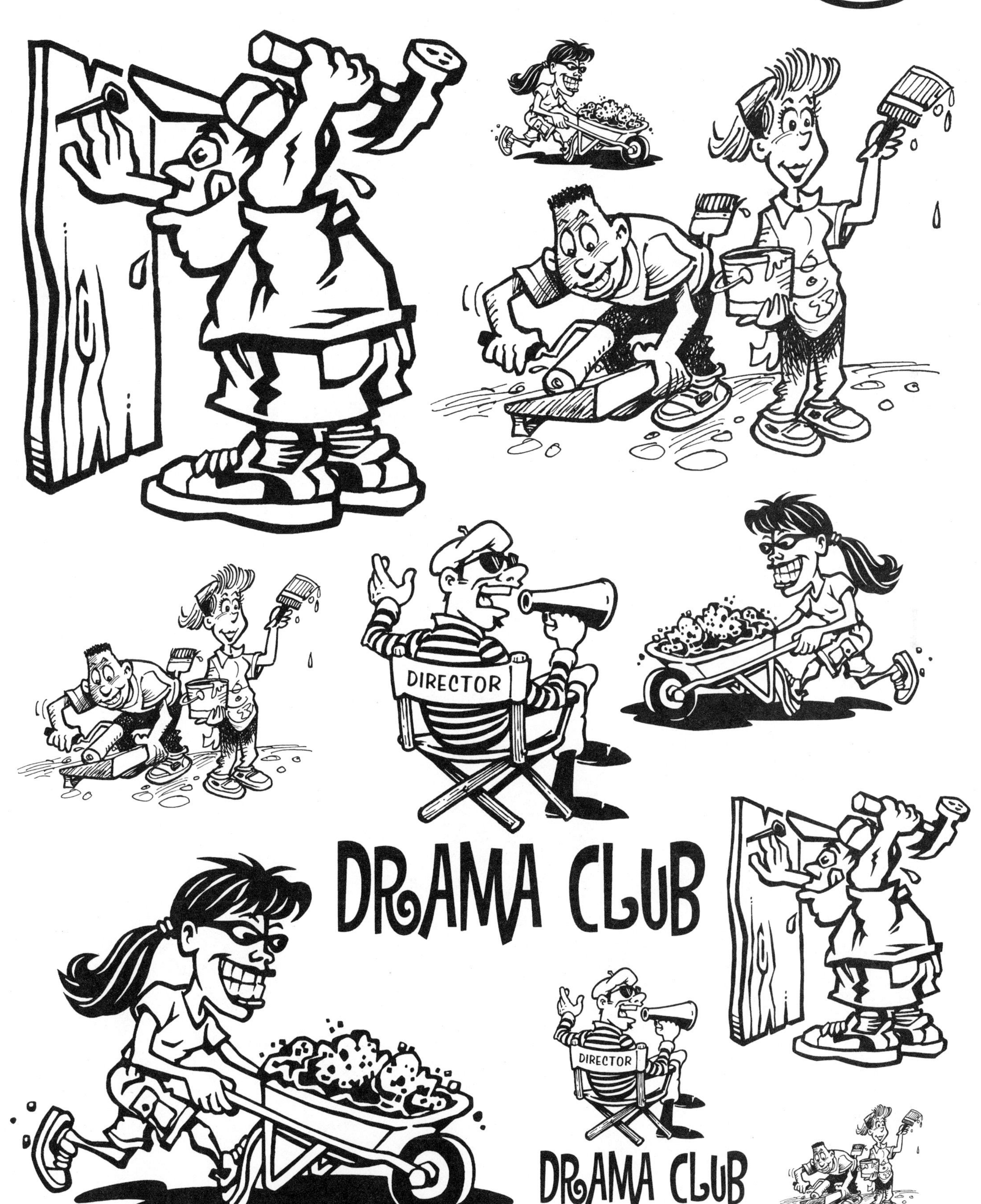
DIRECTOR
DRAMA CLUB
DIRECTOR
DRAMA CLUB

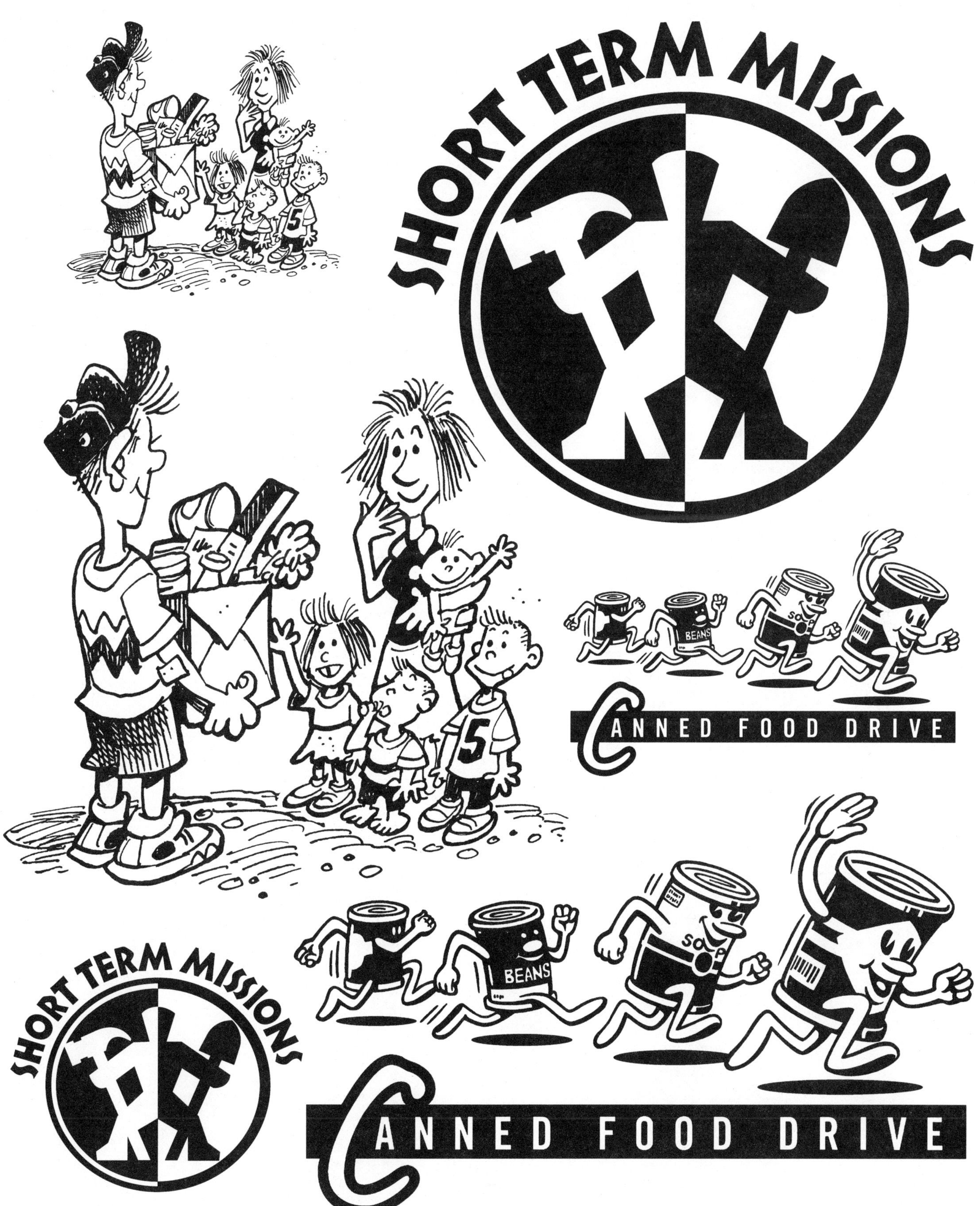
SHORT TERM MISSIONS
BEANS
SOUP
CANNED FOOD DRIVE
BEANS
SOUP
SHORT TERM MISSIONS
CANNED FOOD DRIVE

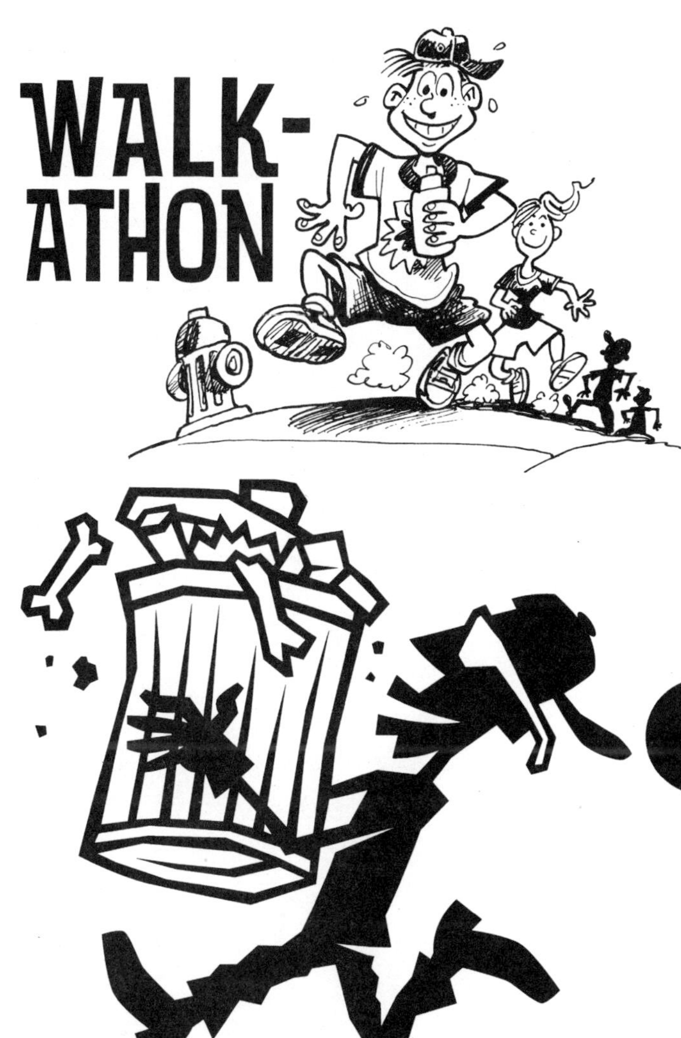

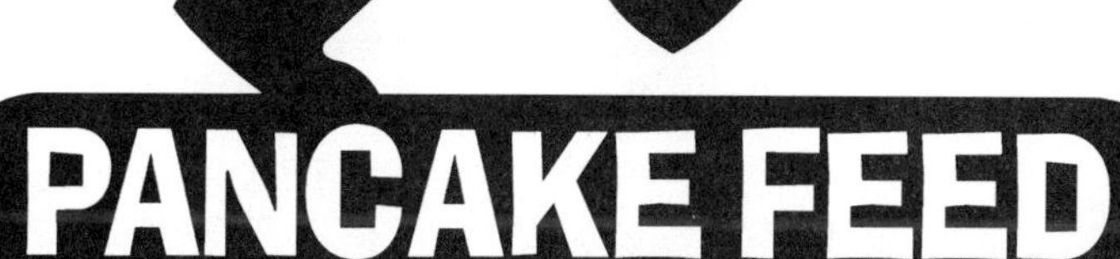

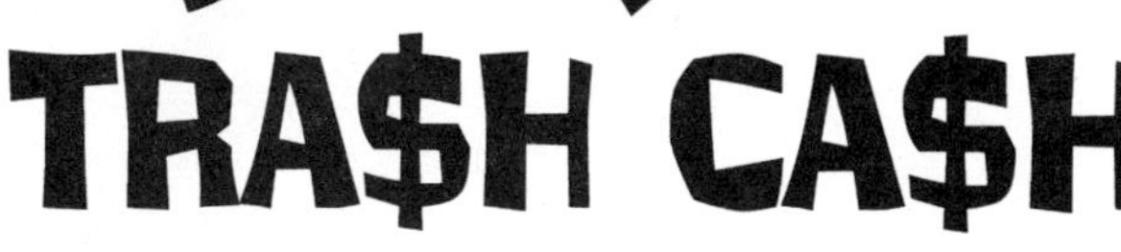

PANCAKE FEED

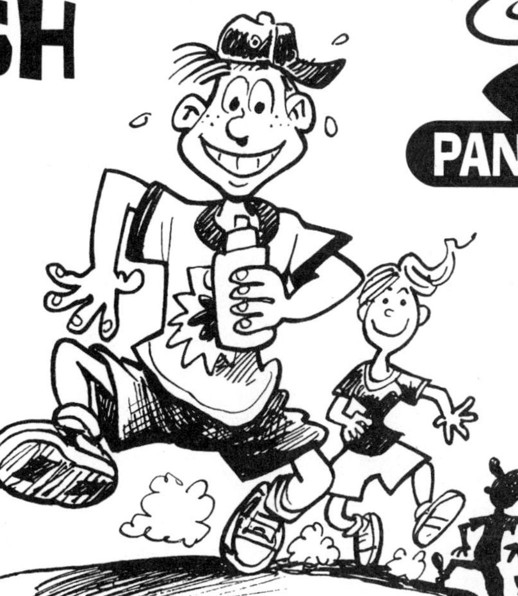

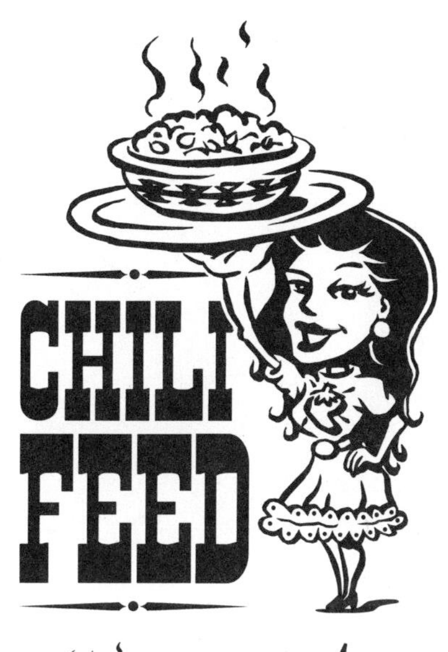
CHILI
FEED

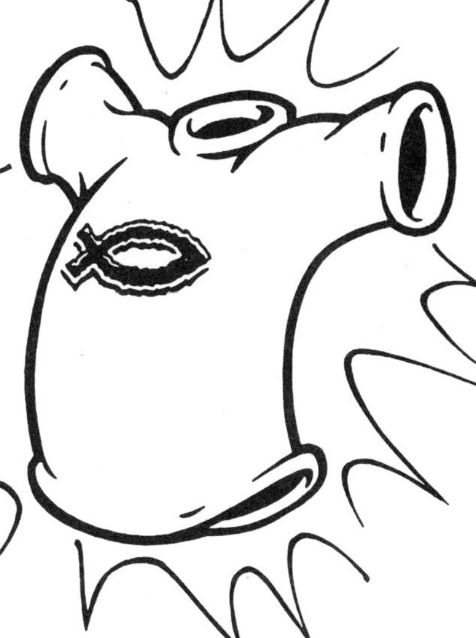
T-SHIRT
Sale

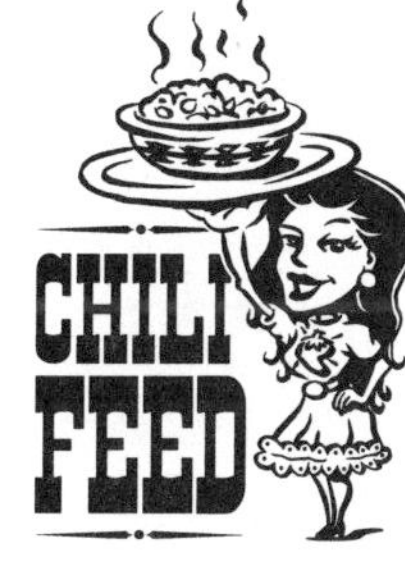
CHILI
FEED

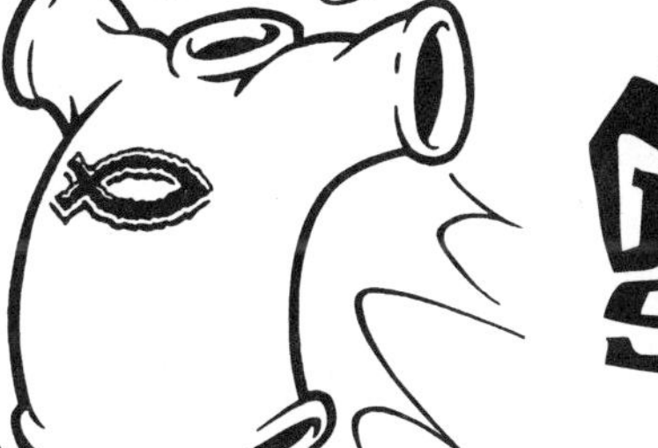
T-SHIRT
Sale

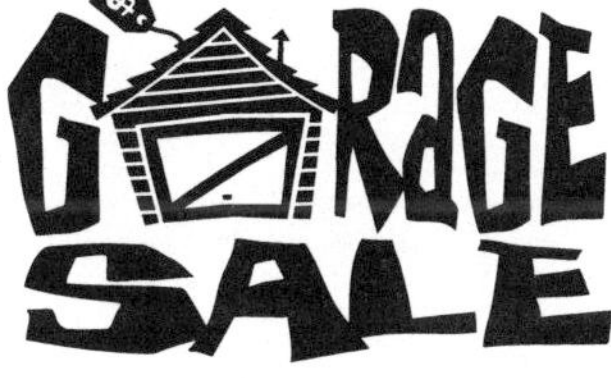
GARAGE
SALE

GARAGE
SALE

GARAGE
SALE

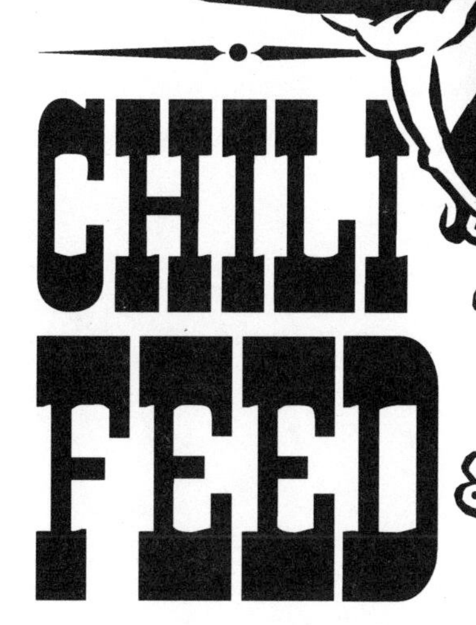
CHILI
FEED

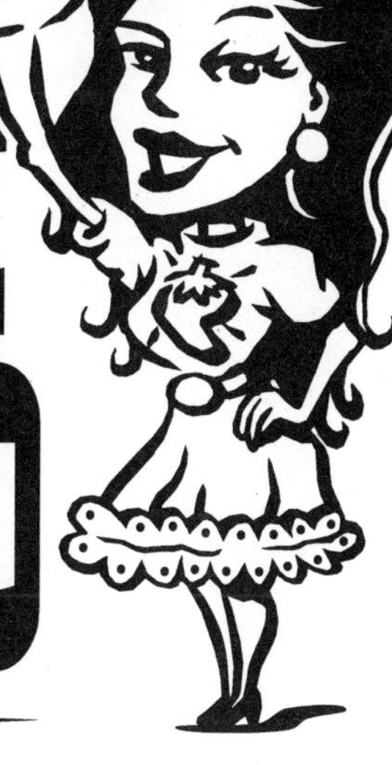

RENT
a
KID
RENT
a
KID
$LAVE $ALE!
RENT
a
KID
RENT
a
KID

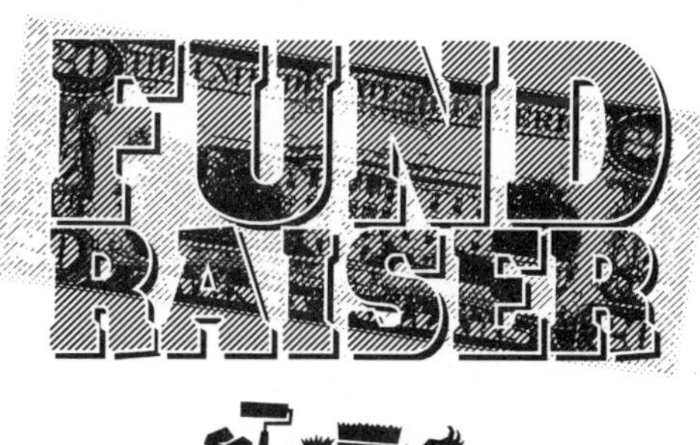
FUND
RAISER

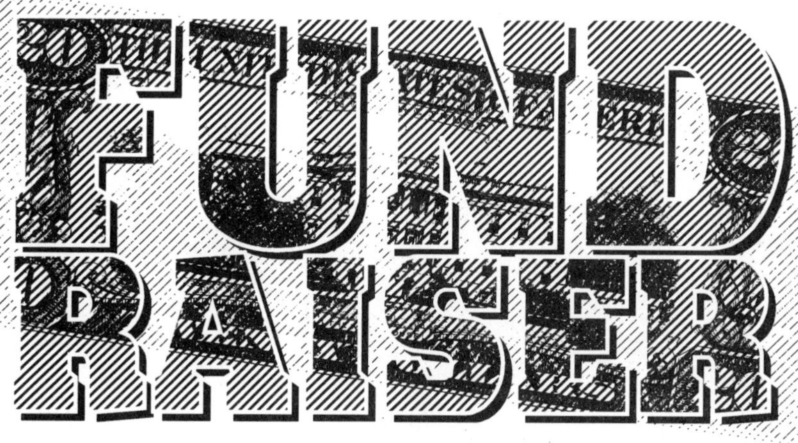
FUND
RAISER

$LAVE $ALE!

$LAVE $ALE!
RENT
a
KID
RENT
a
KID

Spaghetti DINNER

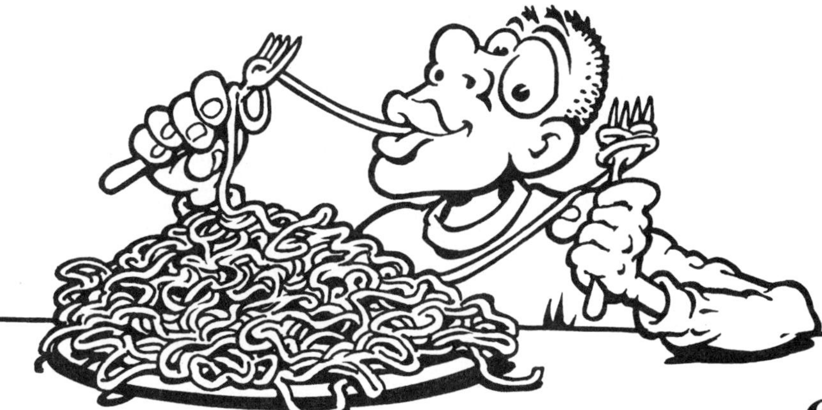

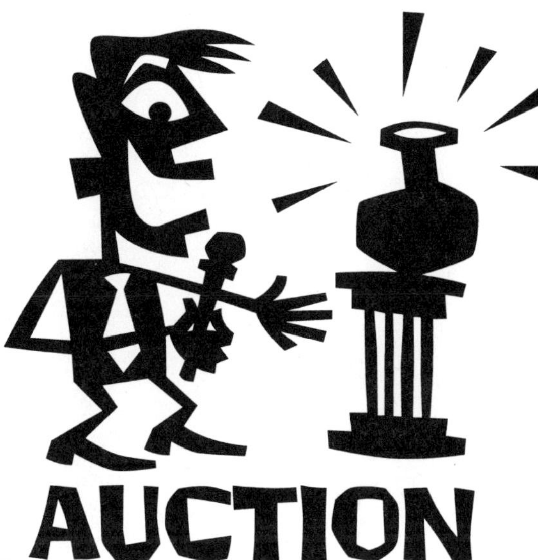

Spaghetti DINNER

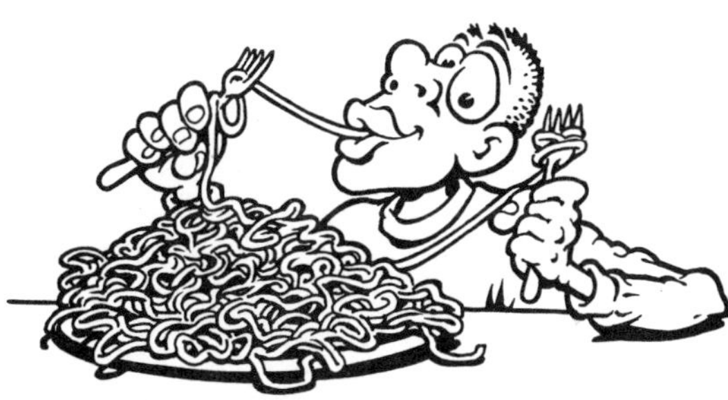

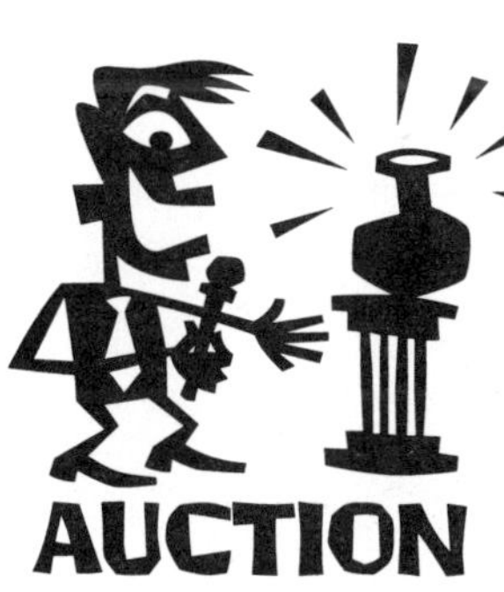

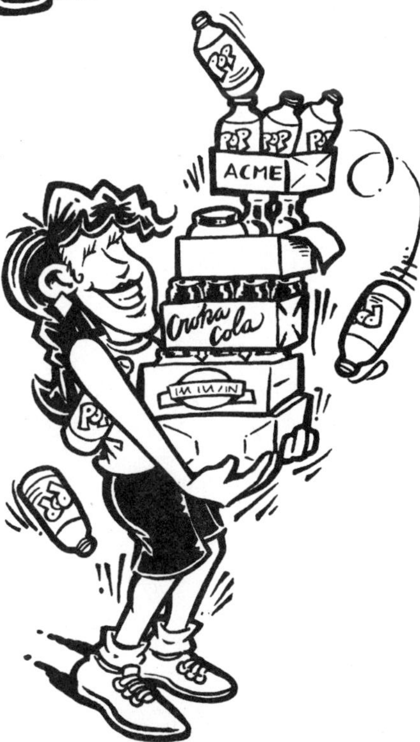

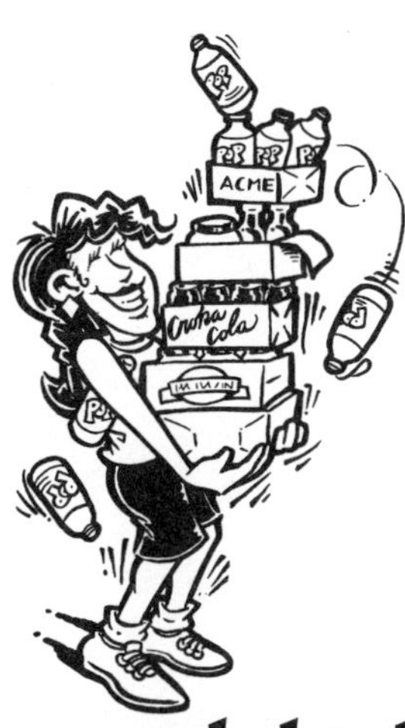

BOTTLE DRIVE

BOTTLE DRIVE

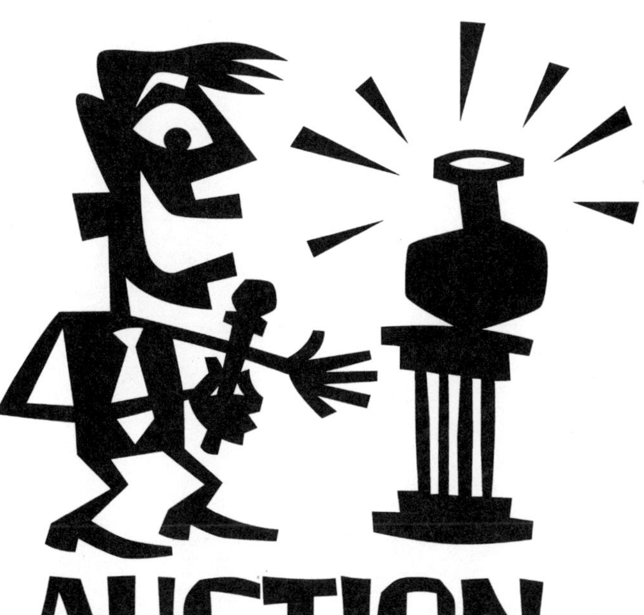

INDEX TO IMAGES

We want to serve you! Send us your ideas so that we can draw them for future books to assist you in your ministry.

Name ______________________________

Church or Ministry ______________________________

Address ______________________________

City ______________________________

State ______________________ Zip ____________

Phone ______________________________

E-mail ______________________________

BRAINSTORM FORM

Here are some ideas I'd like to see in future books:

Food Fun:

Fundraisers:

Group Stuff:

Music:

Summer:

Winter:

Copy and send to : Church Art Works™ • 890 Promontory Place SE • Salem, Oregon 97302 • (503) 370-9377 • FAX (503) 362-5231
E-mail: Info@ChurchArtWorks.com

Youth Specialties Titles

Professional Resources
Administration, Publicity, & Fundraising (Ideas Library)
Developing Student Leaders
Equipped to Serve: Volunteer Youth Worker Training Course
Help! I'm a Junior High Youth Worker!
Help! I'm a Small-Group Leader!
Help! I'm a Sunday School Teacher!
Help! I'm a Volunteer Youth Worker!
How to Expand Your Youth Ministry
How to Speak to Youth...and Keep Them Awake at the Same Time
Junior High Ministry (Updated & Expanded)
The Ministry of Nurture: A Youth Worker's Guide to Discipling Teenagers
One Kid at a Time: Reaching Youth through Mentoring
Purpose-Driven Youth Ministry
So That's Why I Keep Doing This! 52 Devotional Stories for Youth Workers
A Youth Ministry Crash Course
The Youth Worker's Handbook to Family Ministry

Youth Ministry Programming
Camps, Retreats, Missions, & Service Ideas (Ideas Library)
Compassionate Kids: Practical Ways to Involve Your Students in Mission and Service
Creative Bible Lessons from the Old Testament
Creative Bible Lessons in 1 & 2 Corinthians
Creative Bible Lessons in John: Encounters with Jesus
Creative Bible Lessons in Romans: Faith on Fire!
Creative Bible Lessons on the Life of Christ
Creative Junior High Programs from A to Z, Vol. 1 (A-M)
Creative Junior High Programs from A to Z, Vol. 2 (N-Z)
Creative Meetings, Bible Lessons, & Worship Ideas (Ideas Library)
Crowd Breakers & Mixers (Ideas Library)
Drama, Skits, & Sketches (Ideas Library)
Drama, Skits, & Sketches 2 (Ideas Library)
Dramatic Pauses
Everyday Object Lessons
Games (Ideas Library)
Games 2 (Ideas Library)
Great Fundraising Ideas for Youth Groups
More Great Fundraising Ideas for Youth Groups
Great Retreats for Youth Groups
Greatest Skits on Earth
Greatest Skits on Earth, Vol. 2
Holiday Ideas (Ideas Library)
Hot Illustrations for Youth Talks
More Hot Illustrations for Youth Talks
Still More Hot Illustrations for Youth Talks
Incredible Questionnaires for Youth Ministry
Junior High Game Nights
More Junior High Game Nights
Kickstarters: 101 Ingenious Intros to Just about Any Bible Lesson
Live the Life! Student Evangelism Training Kit
Memory Makers
Play It! Great Games for Groups
Play It Again! More Great Games for Groups
Special Events (Ideas Library)
Spontaneous Melodramas
Super Sketches for Youth Ministry
Teaching the Bible Creatively
Videos That Teach
What Would Jesus Do? Youth Leader's Kit
WWJD—The Next Level
Wild Truth Bible Lessons
Wild Truth Bible Lessons 2
Wild Truth Bible Lessons—Pictures of God
Worship Services for Youth Groups

Discussion Starter Resources
Discussion & Lesson Starters (Ideas Library)
Discussion & Lesson Starters 2 (Ideas Library)
Get 'Em Talking
Keep 'Em Talking!
High School TalkSheets
More High School TalkSheets
High School TalkSheets: Psalms and Proverbs
Junior High TalkSheets
More Junior High TalkSheets
Junior High TalkSheets: Psalms and Proverbs
What If...? 450 Thought-Provoking Questions to Get Teenagers Talking, Laughing, and Thinking
Would You Rather...? 465 Provocative Questions to Get Teenagers Talking
Have You Ever...? 450 Intriguing Questions Guaranteed to Get Teenagers Talking

Clip Art
ArtSource: Stark Raving Clip Art (print)
ArtSource: Youth Group Activities (print)
ArtSource CD-ROM: Clip Art Library Version 2.0

Video
EdgeTV
The Heart of Youth Ministry: A Morning with Mike Yaconelli
Next Time I Fall in Love Video Curriculum
Understanding Your Teenager Video Curriculum

Student Books
Grow For It Journal
Grow For It Journal through the Scriptures
Teen Devotional Bible
What Would Jesus Do? Spiritual Challenge Journal
WWJD Spiritual Challenge Journal: The Next Level
Wild Truth Journal for Junior Highers
Wild Truth Journal—Pictures of God